The Winterthur Story

THE HENRY FRANCIS DU PONT WINTERTHUR MUSEUM

THE ARTS IN AMERICA

By EDGAR P. RICHARDSON

Winterthur is a newcomer in the world of museums. Its collections are famous wherever American decorative arts are known and collected; but its nature and purposes as an institution are far from being generally understood. The purpose of this first number of the *Winterthur Portfolio* is to present our institution, its past history, its present program, the contribution we hope to make to American studies and useful knowledge.

The building which houses the museum, and the surrounding park, are the result of a century and a quarter of growth. The collections were begun forty years ago by Mr. H. F. du Pont. The museum was organized, however, only in 1951 and its staff and activities have since grown so rapidly that anyone may be forgiven for unfamiliarity with Winterthur as an institution. The Winterthur collections are also, by location and manner of display, somewhat difficult of access. The *Portfolio* is part of an effort to make them more accessible by a varied range of publications.

The collections at Winterthur are outstanding as a representation of two hundred years of activity by the artists and craftsmen of the American colonies and early republic, covering the period roughly from 1640 to 1840. This is a field of art well known to collectors but not at all familiar to the non-collector. As life precedes history, so the artist and the collector precede the historian; works of art are created, and collected, before they are studied. It is no exaggeration to say that the story of the artists and craftsmen of this country, and the meaning of their work, are still in general most imperfectly known. We are in need of more accurately detailed knowledge and of wider generalization based upon that knowledge, before these arts can take their place in history or throw, as only the arts can, their penetrating light upon our civilization.

How large a body of evidence do they represent? The first documented commission given an American craftsman is, so far as we know, that given by the General Court of Massachusetts Bay Colony in 1652 to John Hull to set up a mint at Boston for the coining of shillings. The dies from which they struck their coins were obtained from Joseph Jenks of Lynn, the first iron founder of Massachusetts.[1] A Pine-Tree Shilling minted by John Hull and Robert Sanderson is in our collection. The first documented commission to an American painter was given by Governor Peter Stuyvesant of New Netherland to Hendrick Couturier, formerly a member of the painters' guild of Leyden, who was, so far as is known, the first European-trained portrait painter to practice in this country. Couturier had emigrated to America by 1661, or earlier, and settled at New Amstel (New Castle) on the Delaware River, but was active also in New Amsterdam (New York) on the North River. The June 12, 1663, minutes of an executive session of the Burgomasters of New Amsterdam record that the wife of Hendrick Couturier testified "her husband had painted the portrait of his Honour [Petrus Stuyvesant] and drawn pictures of his sons." Her husband was at this time "a merchant at New Amstel on the South River."[2] Unfortunately none of Couturier's work seems to have survived, either at Winterthur or elsewhere.

In the centuries that follow, thousands of artists and craftsmen, both men and women with skilled hands, keen eyes, and gifted brains, gave us an

---

[1] *American Silver of the Work of Seventeenth and Eighteenth Century Silversmiths exhibited at the Museum of Fine Arts, June to November, 1906,* Boston, 1906, p. 13.

[2] I. N. PHELPS STOKES, *The Iconography of Manhattan Island,* 1922, IV, 225 and 1915, I, 95.

immense, varied, and significant heritage. The *Dictionary of American Biography* has great merits, but its coverage of artists is spotty and of craftsmen nil. *The New-York Historical Society's Dictionary of Artists in America 1564-1860* limits itself to painters, sculptors, and engravers of that period: the total number of names listed is between ten and eleven thousand. The index of the Archives of American Art now lists over 20,-000 names, and the number grows rapidly. It is evident that there is a sufficient body of evidence to attract and deserve the curiosity of historians of American civilization, other than art historians. We hope that the *Winterthur Portfolio* may prove useful to them.

Other aspects of the life of the arts in American society are also significant. The migration of works of art into America began with the first settlers of the seventeenth century. The Venetian glass found in excavations at Jamestown, Governor John Winthrop's portrait painted during a visit to England and brought to Massachusetts Bay on his return, represent the beginning of the importation of artistic treasure to this country for use, pleasure, and reflection. The importation of works of art for use in American homes is well represented in our collection. The more subtle and intangible migration of ideas—the heritage of artistic forms which form the background and point of departure of creative effort—is represented both in the works of art themselves and by the design books in the hands of the craftsmen.

The impact of this continent, so vast, so unlike anything in the previous experience of our ancestors, began to make itself felt with the first explorer-artists, Jacques Le Moyne de Morgues, who visited Florida in 1564-65, and John White, who came several times to Roanoke in the years 1585-93. Its influence is all pervasive yet as impalpable as the air we breathe; the questions it raises are important, difficult, elusive.

The material we propose to discuss in this periodical is the story of the arts and crafts in America, considered as material noble and interesting in itself and as a significant document for all students of civilization. We have chosen the title the *Winterthur Portfolio* partly in recognition of the fact that our publication will by nature be a miscellany, partly in memory of an earlier journal. The *Portfolio* founded in Philadelphia in 1801 was in the period of the early republic what *Harper's, Scribner's* and the *Century* were to the United States in the later nineteenth century—a periodical of literary quality and humanistic learning, whose illustrations were works of art, and whose contents offered both knowledge and pleasure. We hope to make our *Portfolio* also a vehicle of humanistic learning, substantial in its information, but giving pleasure also by its form and style. And while it is evident from what I have said that the basis for our journal is the immense collections at Winterthur, we can draw no narrow or exact frontiers for the explorations and studies which we may publish. Ideas, or works of art, even if created or expressed at an exact moment in history, have a way of escaping from temporal limits and of floating freely, mysteriously on the stream of time. What we see and judge in a work of art is the creative process of the man who made it, embodied in a form that endures. The inanimate object comes alive *as a work of art* when it wakes a response in the mind of a living observer. That is the meaning of Croce's observation that all art is contemporary art, since it is alive as a fresh experience in the life of each one of us, and history is the present day's interpretation of that experience.

The arts in America as shown at Winterthur are symbolized by six matching silver tankards made about 1772 by the Boston silversmith and patriot, Paul Revere. Each is inscribed "The Gift of Mary Bartlett, Widow of Eph^m Bartlett, to the third Church in Brookfeild. 1768," and is marked •REVERE in rectangle, with its original weight scratched on the base. In the extant account books of Paul Revere in the Massachusetts Historical Society, only one set of six tankards is recorded.

History of the Winterthur Estate

By E. McCLUNG FLEMING

"WINTERTHUR" is a name with many associations. There is the du Pont family, for five generations associated with the Brandywine Valley and one of the most brilliant industrial achievements in American history. There is the estate, for nearly one hundred and fifty years in the same family, beginning as 450 acres in 1818, growing to 2,400 acres in 1926, now 1,100 acres, and always beautiful with its wheat and corn fields, meadows, streams, and woodlands. There is the one hundred and twenty-five-year-old main building, from 1839 until 1951 a private residence, and from 1951 a public museum; since 1930 rising nine stories and extending through 150 rooms. There are the farm, with its dairy herd, and the world-renowned gardens, both dating from 1839, and each known to scores of experts who may know little about the museum. There is the forty-year-old collection of the American arts and the twelve-year-old museum which has grown into a center of advanced study of the early American arts and culture. And finally, there is the moving spirit, Henry Francis du Pont, representing the fifth generation of the family to live in this valley. "Winterthur" means all these things.

Plans for Winterthur, as a new home for Antoine Bidermann and his wife Evelina Gabrielle du Pont, were probably made in 1833, the land for it purchased in 1837, and the new residence begun in 1839. Through the Bidermanns, Winterthur was, from the start, an intimate part of the du Pont world on the Brandywine. For twenty years Antoine had been the chief business associate of Eleuthère Irénée du Pont, founder of the powder company, and for another two and a half years had been his successor as executive head of the company. Evelina was the second daughter of Eleuthère Irénée and one of seven children, all of whom lived under their father's roof or in homes close by. The Bidermanns' home from their marriage in 1816 until 1837 was Hagley House above the Brandywine, overlooking the powder mills. The land they purchased for Winterthur had been first acquired by E. I. du Pont, had for more than twenty-five years been part of his farming and sheep-raising operations, and was purchased from his heirs. When, therefore, in 1839, Antoine and Evelina Bidermann moved their home from the Brandywine to Winterthur, it was only a move from one part of the familiar family holdings to another not two and a half miles away.

Fig. 1
The Bidermann Family,
c. 1795, *From left:*
James Antoine,
Gabrielle Aimée Odier,
Marie Jacqueline,
Jacques Franklin,
and Jacques Antoine
Bidermann. Oil portrait.
Coll. Jacques-Edmond
Bidermann, Paris.

The first master of Winterthur, James Antoine Bidermann (known in Delaware as Antoine Bidermann) was born in Paris in 1790. He was the eldest son of Jacques Antoine Bidermann, a Swiss millionaire businessman and banker then living in France, and Gabrielle Aimée Odier, daughter of a prominent citizen of Geneva (Fig. 1). The Bidermanns were an old, distinguished Swiss family, having established themselves at Winterthur in the sixteenth century. They were French, and Protestant.[1] The father, son of Hans Jacob Bidermann, Senator from Winterthur, had fled Switzerland in 1782 for political reasons, building up an international business empire first in Brussels and after 1789 in Paris. The following year he became a

---

[1] CHARLES POISSON, *Les Fournisseurs Aux Armées Sons la Revolution Francaise* (Paris: Libraire Historique A. Margraff, 1932), pp. 33-34.

Fig. 2 James Antoine Bidermann
in 1816, *miniature.*
*Coll. Jacques-Edmond Bidermann,
Paris.*

Fig. 3
Eleuthère Irénée du Pont
in 1831, *oil portrait
by Rembrandt Peale.
Coll. Irénée du Pont
(photo. E. I. du Pont
de Nemours and Company).*

French citizen, formed a wide circle of influential friends, and was appointed to a succession of municipal and state offices. In 1791, he was able to put nearly six million francs at the disposal of the impoverished French government, and in 1804 he loaned four million to Napoleon.[2] As the French Revolution erupted into violence, young Bidermann was sent by his father to the family home at Winterthur, Switzerland, where an uncle gave him useful business training. He returned to Paris in 1804 to assist in his father's business enterprises.

One of his father's investments was in Du Pont de Nemours, Père, Fils et Cie., a stock company organized by Pierre Samuel du Pont to invest in American land development. In 1798, French capitalists were invited to purchase stock in the company, and Bidermann was one of the first and largest subscribers; in 1808, he was listed as owning 13 out of 36 shares.[3] Moreover in 1801, when du Pont's son Eleuthère Irénée sought French support for a new gunpowder manufactory on the Brandywine, Bidermann became one of the original four incorporators and one of the six principal stockholders. However, in 1811 du Pont's company failed, by 1814 no dividend had been paid by the American powder works, and ugly rumors were circulating to the effect that its head, Eleuthère Irénée du Pont, was deliberately cheating the stockholders. With the older du Pont's approval, the French stockholders decided to send young Bidermann over to the Brandywine to get the facts.

James Antoine, now twenty-four years old (Fig. 2), was glad to come to the United States on this mission. It would give him an opportunity to visit friends in Kentucky where his father had once owned 56,000 acres of land, to find an occupation, and possibly to establish a home. Among several letters of introduction which he brought with him, two were written by Lafayette to Thomas Jefferson and Bushrod Washington. After a long voyage interrupted by stops in the Azores, Halifax, Providence, and Philadelphia, young Bidermann arrived at Wilmington on August 8, 1814. He immediately plunged into a thorough study of the Company's records, cordially being given free access to all papers by Irénée du Pont (Fig. 3).

[2] Leo Weisz, "Die Biedermann und New-Winterthur," *Neue Zuericher Zeitung.* June 8, 1952.
[3] Bessie Gardner du Pont, *E. I. du Pont de Nemours and Company: A History* (New York: Houghton Mifflin Company, 1920), p. 181.

Fig. 4
Evelina Gabrielle du Pont, in 1813,
oil portrait by Rembrandt Peale.
Coll. Mme. Georges Hueber, Paris.

It was a dramatic moment for the powder company. Basically, the latter was a solid success, having been greatly aided by government contracts for powder during the war of 1812; indeed, since 1810 it had been the largest powder manufactory on this side of the Atlantic. However, though Eleuthère Irénée had been able to handle the administrative and engineering problems very well, his vexing financial problems had been complicated by the business failures of both his father and his brother Victor; adverse action now by the French stockholders might prove extremely embarrassing. Fortunately, young Bidermann had enough business acumen to recognize ability and integrity when he saw them, and within a week he had found out enough to send his father a report clearing the company of all charges of unfairness.

With equal rapidity young Bidermann won the complete confidence of Irénée. Within a few days of his arrival, the harassed powder manufacturer could write to his stepsister that Bidermann's arrival was "a very fortunate thing" for him. By October, 1814, he was invited to make his home with the du Pont family, and in February, 1815, he joined Irénée in buying Pierre Bauduy's interest in the Company, assuming the latter's position and duties there as Irénée's sole business partner.[4] Seven months later he married Irénée's daughter, Evelina Gabrielle.

The match pleased everyone. Young Antoine Bidermann shared his bride's French background. He had certainly won his spurs, having been for over a year the trusted partner of his father-in-law, as well as one of four partners holding stock in a tannery and morocco factory located on the Brandywine at Hagley.[5] Moreover, Evelina's grandfather and Antoine's father were good friends and business associates, and were glad to see the families united. Pierre Samuel du Pont had been among the first French visitors to frequent Jacques Bidermann's new Paris home in 1789,

[4] *Ibid.*, p. 50.
[5] BESSIE GARDNER DU PONT, *Life of Eleuthère Irénée du Pont From Contemporary Correspondence 1819-1834* (Newark, Delaware: University of Delaware Press, 1926), X, 126, XI, 251-257.

and the two shared similar views on politics and economics. Both men enrolled in the National Guard, both were friends of Mirabeau; while du Pont was serving in the National Assembly as a moderate delegate from Nemours, Bidermann was being elected a moderate Paris alderman, then Town Councilman of Paris, and soon a key member of the government ministry of supply. Furthermore, the latter established in Paris a liberal journal to which du Pont, a fellow physiocrat, contributed.[6]

Evelina (Fig. 4), known affectionately to relatives and friends as "Lena," was born in Paris in 1796. She was a serious, family-centered young lady with a taste for literature and a modest skill in sketching, who could hardly have failed to be impressed by the tactful, capable young Frenchman. When, therefore, young Antoine asked Evelina's hand in marriage, everyone on both sides of the family approved. Evelina's illness in the spring of 1816 delayed the marriage, but on September 14 the wedding took place, the Episcopal rites being conducted by the Rev. William Wickes, Rector of Old Swedes Church. The groom was then twenty-six years old, the bride twenty.

The du Pont family, in the midst of which the young Bidermanns started their married life, was a large, cosmopolitan, and close-knit one, centering in the households of the two brothers, Eleuthère Irénée and Victor Marie. At Eleutherian Mills, on the west bank of the Brandywine, Irénée's household included his wife Sophie and his seven children—three of them born in Paris and four of them here. Victor's household, living across the Brandywine at Louviers, included his wife Josephine de Pelleport and their four children. Other homes were soon added. In 1824, Nemours was built for Alfred Victor, adjacent to Eleutherian Mills, and here his seven children were born; in 1836, Rokeby was built for Gabrielle Josephine du Pont at the time of her marriage.

From May, 1815, until August, 1817, the little community also included Pierre Samuel du Pont de Nemours, father of Victor and Irénée and patriarch of the household. His career had been a notable one. Economist, publicist, and statesman, he had been an acquaintance of Diderot, the older Mirabeau, Voltaire, and Talleyrand, the protégé of the great physiocrats François Quesnay and Turgot, and close friend of Benjamin Franklin and Thomas Jefferson. His far-ranging interests included natural science, philosophy, education, manufacturing methods, agriculture, and metaphysics. During the French Revolution, he had suffered the fate of an active constitutional monarchist, being at one time imprisoned and sentenced to the guillotine, and later sentenced to deportation with his house sacked and his printing press destroyed. It was in this extremity that he had, in 1799, brought his household to the United States for a fresh start. However, in 1802, while Irénée was laying the foundations for the powder manufactory on the Brandywine, the elder du Pont had returned to France. The restoration of Louis XVIII led to fresh honors: appointment as secretary to the provisional government, Chevalier of the Legion of Honor, and a Counsellor of State. But on Napoleon's return from Elba, Pierre Samuel again fled France to rejoin his children on the Brandywine. Advisor to several kings and one American president, a man of warm enthusiasms, unquenchable optimism, and many friendships, his presence was for two years a rich addition to the lives of his children and grandchildren. His death in

---

[6] WEISZ, loc. cit.

1817 was due to over-zealous participation in a bucket brigade putting out a fire in the charcoal house, and young Bidermann was one of two watching over him when he died.[7] Pierre Samuel du Pont lies buried in the family cemetery above the Brandywine. Coincidentally, Antoine made strenuous efforts to have his own father join him at Hagley, but Bidermann senior also died in 1817.

For eighteen years, Evelina and Antoine Bidermann made their home in the midst of the family and company activities at Hagley House, a frame building erected by Irénée in 1814 for the director of the mills. A sketch done in 1822 by C. A. LeSueur, the French artist and naturalist, shows the porch with its fine view of the Brandywine and the textile mill which is now the Hagley Museum. Bidermann's stable must have been a roomy one, for it was later removed to Squirrel Run and served as an armory during the Civil War. The Bidermann bath house, as a "domestic bathing arrangement in a separate building" was one of the earliest mentioned in the Delaware Valley.[8]

Life at Hagley House was simple and economical, but never dull. An only child, James Irénée, was born there in 1817; from Paris, Mrs. Pierre Samuel du Pont de Nemours sent "a thousand benedictions to my Lena's baby." The powder company brought a stream of visitors—technical experts, business men, politicians. And Irénée, as a cultured gentleman of his day, had agricultural and scientific interests which kept his home filled with visitors. The Bidermanns must have joined in the welcome to Lafayette in 1824, when he made two visits to Wilmington and stayed at both Eleutherian Mills and Louviers; and to Henry Clay in 1833 when he visited at Eleutherian Mills. In October, 1827, the Bidermanns made a year-long trip to Europe, the first of three, combining family and company business. Antoine visited his widowed mother in Winterthur, Switzerland, while Evelina sought treatment for a severe injury she had sustained. Antoine was known affectionately as "Brother" in Irénée's household, and Alfred Victor named his youngest son Antoine Bidermann after him.

As Irénée's only partner from 1815 until 1834, Bidermann had an active and responsible role in helping to run the powder company. According to the initial articles of agreement he was to give "as much time as necessary to the business of manufacture, the purchase of materials, the sale of powder, the establishment of agencies and magazines in the interior of the country, and to the adjustment of accounts." [9] Soon he was undertaking company trips to New York, Boston, Nashville, Louisville. The frequent explosions in the powder mills deeply stirred his humanitarian sense, and in his first year he advocated the then radical policy of pensioning families that had suffered. Personable, industrious, and astute, he proved to be a good representative of the Company, and steadily grew in influence. To Irénée he was, for nearly twenty years, an intimate friend and confidant to whom the harassed business man would turn for help when "the blue devils" got him. Irénée loved him as a son, and when in 1828 his wife Sophie died,

[7] WILLIAM S. DUTTON, *Du Pont: One Hundred and Forty Years* (New York: Charles Scribner's Sons, 1942), p. 55-56; SOPHIE M. DU PONT, "Souveniers of Brother," The Henry Francis du Pont Winterthur MSS Collection, Eleutherian Mills Historical Library (hereafter cited as EMHL).

[8] LOUISE DU PONT CROWNINSHIELD and PIERRE S. DU PONT, "Explanatory Notes" *The Tancopanican Chronicle* (Wilmington, Delaware, 1950), p. 4.

[9] RALPH D. GRAY, "Biographical Sketch of J. A. Bidermann" (unpublished report, Hagley Museum, 1957), p. 9.

he was glad, in his grief and loss, to let Bidermann handle all the business. When Irénée himself died suddenly in 1834, Bidermann's long experience with all phases of the Company's business made him the logical choice as the next executive head until young Alfred du Pont could be trained for the position. Consequently, from November 1, 1834, Bidermann was the senior partner and chief executive of the firm, demonstrating skillful financial management during a three-year period of great national and Company prosperity. Antoine Bidermann, Walter S. Carpenter, and Crawford Greenewalt have been the only three heads of the Company born outside the du Pont family.

Bidermann undertook the direction of the Company in 1834 with the clear intention of carrying out two of Irénées fondest dreams: that his sons would eventually continue his leadership of the Company, and that all notes still held by French stockholders should be paid in full. Both objectives took careful planning, and both were carried out with characteristic tact and skill. Under his able tutelage, Alfred completed his managerial apprenticeship by the spring of 1837, and Bidermann then reorganized the firm with the three brothers as the active partners, and the four sisters as the "sleeping" partners, Alfred becoming senior partner. Evelina remained a partner until 1850. By the same date, Bidermann was ready to pay off the French creditors, and he arranged a trip to France to do this in person. While in France, he would also check on recent gunpowder manufacturing techniques and report these to Alfred. On April 1, Antoine's resignation from the Company and the inauguration of the new partnership took effect. The Bidermanns then purchased two shares of the new stock, loaned the three du Pont brothers $56,000, and in August sailed with their son to France on the *Burgundy*. Soon the last dollar was paid the remaining French stockholders, and technical reports were coming in to Alfred.[10] Antoine Bidermann had completed his services to E. I. du Pont de Nemours and Company, and now turned to a career as a gentleman farmer at Winterthur.

The spring of 1837 was a turning point for the Bidermanns. The two were financially independent: Antoine had inherited his father's shares of du Pont stock in 1817, Evelina received her inheritance from Irénée's estate in 1834, and these shares were appreciating. Antoine had done all he could for Irénée, and then for Irénée's three sons, and his services were not needed now as they had been before. It was also time for the Bidermanns to leave Hagley House and to acquire a home of their own more suitable to their means. The decision to turn from manufacturing to farming may not have been too difficult, but the question whether to take up farming in this country or in France was not settled on their departure. Bidermann's ties to France were strong, his son seemed to be leaning toward a career there, and his mother lived as a widow in Switzerland.

After two months in Europe, the Bidermanns knew that they wished to return to Delaware and build a home and a farm on the land they had purchased before sailing. This land consisted of 450 acres and was admirably suited for the development of a fine estate. Made up of four adjoining

[10] BESSIE GARDNER DU PONT, *E. I. du Pont de Nemours and Company*, p. 59; DUTTON, p. 68; GEORGE H. KERR, *Du Pont Romance* (Wilmington, Delaware: Du Pont Printing Division, 1938), p. 5; J. A. Bidermann to Henry du Pont, January 30, 1838, Old Stone Office Records, The E. I. du Pont de Nemours and Company Collection, EMHL.

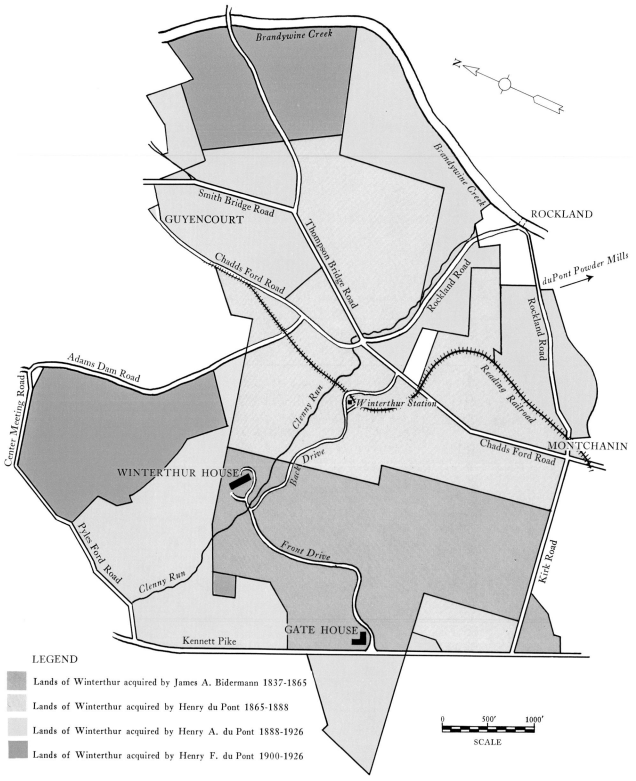

Brandywine Creek

ROCKLAND

duPont Powder Mills

Smith Bridge Road

GUYENCOURT

Thompson Bridge Road

Chadds Ford Road

Rockland Road

Rockland Road

Adams Dam Road

Center Meeting Road

Clenny Run

Winterthur Station

Reading Railroad

MONTCHANIN

Chadds Ford Road

WINTERTHUR HOUSE

Back Drive

Pyles Ford Road

Front Drive

Kirk Road

Clenny Run

Kennett Pike

GATE HOUSE

LEGEND

Lands of Winterthur acquired by James A. Bidermann 1837-1865

Lands of Winterthur acquired by Henry du Pont 1865-1888

Lands of Winterthur acquired by Henry A. du Pont 1888-1926

Lands of Winterthur acquired by Henry F. du Pont 1900-1926

0   500'   1000'

SCALE

Fig. 5 Winterthur, 1837-1927, *drawing by Leslie Potts, 1963, Winterthur Museum.*

parcels which had been acquired by Irénée du Pont between 1810 and 1818, the property had been inherited jointly by his seven children at his death in 1834, and was put up for sale in January 1837. On April 4, the Bidermanns purchased it. It is possible that they had thought of this tract even before Irénée's death. Early in October, Antoine wrote Alfred Victor from Paris, "I am more than ever decided to end my days near you. . . . . I shall not feel *at home* except near the Brandywine." Two months later, the decision was confirmed in a letter to Henry: "I'm more resolved than ever to establish myself on Clenny Run as soon as the fixed term of my visit will have expired here."

Once certain that he would return to Delaware, Bidermann immediately plunged into the details of planning his new home and farm, and in this he had the able collaboration of Alfred Victor and Henry du Pont. "If the business goes well next summer," he wrote from Paris in October, "I shall ask you to have built a little house for me on the place I showed you and to buy timber as occasion offers, for building a larger one, so that the wood may have time to dry thoroughly." The "little house" was to be a tenant farm house, and in a series of letters to his brothers-in-law he discussed every detail of the building from floor plans to kitchen, piazza, well, and attic.[11] Similarly for the "larger one," his own residence, he ordered the timber to be cut and seasoned, commissioned floor plans and elevations by the French architect N. Vergnaud, and purchased French windows to be taken home with him.

Meanwhile, in planning his new farm, he studied scientific agricultural techniques, and corresponded with the brothers about soil and animal care. He wrote of spending much time in studying the manufacture of beet sugar on the possibility that it might thrive in the Brandywine Valley as it did in France; he wrote of "many experiments and calculations" he planned to undertake on his lands. "I thank Henry," he wrote Alfred Victor on April 6, 1839, "for the details . . . on Durham cattle and other livestock. From what he says I think that if I want full bred cows it would be better to import them myself than to buy them in America, but for that there must be a stable to receive them and pasture to feed them and I have much to do before all that will be ready. I would like to have when I arrive a good pair of oxen and a cart . . ." The Bidermanns returned, without their son, in May, 1839. Soon the new farmhouse, residence, garden, and farm would be in operation (Fig. 5).

The new estate was located in the northerly portion of Christiana Hundred, about four and a half miles from Wilmington, two from Centerville, and one and a half from the Brandywine. It comprised 450 acres of high, rolling farmland and woodland through which ran the small stream known as "Clenny Run" which originated in Centerville and flowed in a west-east direction through a narrow, mile-long meadow, eventually reaching the Brandywine. Of the four parcels from Irénée's estate in 1837, two were well known locally for the farms located on them. One, in the southeast section of the estate, was known as the Martin Farm. The land had been originally acquired from William Penn by a patent dated February 19, 1692/3 [12] by Richard Gregg of the same family who owned the land on which Eleutherian Mills was later built. Irénée purchased it as a parcel of 181 acres in 1810 and named it "Merino Farm" because of his plan to raise fine specimens of this breed there. It was in 1801 that he had brought back from France the famous pioneer merino ram Don Pedro that remained in

[11] Copies of letters from J. A. Bidermann to Alfred Victor and Henry du Pont, 1838, 1839, The Henry Francis du Pont Winterthur Collection, EMHL.

[12] "Title of Colonel Henry A. du Pont to Winterthur Farm" (typescript in Winterthur Farm Office). Variations in the spelling of "Clenny" in this document include: Cleany, Cleney, Cleneay, Clenney. Elsewhere it is spelled "Cluny."

Fig. 6 James Antoine Bidermann
in 1838, *crayon portrait by Duloc.*
Coll. Jacques-Edmond Bidermann.

Fig. 7 Evelina Gabrielle du Pont
Bidermann in 1838, *crayon portrait*
by Duloc. Coll. Jacques-Edmond Bidermann.

his care from 1805 until 1811. His motive was partly to take advantage of a speculative sales item, since the "Merino mania" was then virulent in Delaware, and partly to supply fine wool for his brother Victor's woolen factory.[13] "This farm can maintain at present 500 sheep," he wrote his father, "and when it will be improved, from 700 to 800 . . . . This at one dollar per pound makes a production of $2000 for a flock of 500, which is a very good result." The farm was placed under the direction of William Martin, "an excellent man" who had worked in the powder yards for eight years and was now happy to turn to farming. The Martin farmhouse is still in service at Winterthur.

The second farm, on which Bidermann built his home, and which therefore came to be the heart of Winterthur, was known as the Clenny Farm, and the little brook that flowed through it Clenny Run. The farmhouse, located on Cadwallader Hill, was retained by Bidermann until 1844.[14] William Clenny had acquired the land from the Penn proprietors in 1741. His son had sold it in 1794 to Rumford Dawes, a Philadelphia Quaker businessman who was then operating three mills on the Brandywine on ground that he had named "Hagley" and which was soon to be purchased by Irénée du Pont for his powder mills. The Clenny Farm was bought by Irénée in 1811 as a parcel of 169 acres. This was the year that the Wilmington and Kennett Turnpike, which ran along the southwest border of the farm, was incorporated. During the War of 1812, partly because of its proximity to the pike, but also because of its water supply and healthy location, the field between the pike and the later front-entrance drive to Winterthur was selected for the site of Camp du Pont, where several units

---

[13] CARROLL W. PURSELL, JR., "E. I. du Pont, Don Pedro, and the Introduction of Merino Sheep into the United States, 1801: A Document," *Agricultural History,* Vol. 33, No. 2, 1959, 86-88; "E. I. du Pont and the Merino Mania in Delaware 1805-1815," *ibid,* Vol. 36, No. 2, 91-100.
[14] Evelina Bidermann to J. I. Bidermann, May 9, 1844, Bidermann Letters (microfilm 55.6), EMHL.

Fig. 8A   Winterthur House, 1839-1884, *from the north.*   Fig. 8B   Winterthur House, 1839-1884, *south elevation.*
   (Photo. Eleutherian Mills Historical Library)   (Photo. Eleutherian Mills Historical Library)

of the Advance Light Brigade of the First Division of Pennsylvania militia
were posted to protect the powder mills. From September 29 to November
30, 1814, the volunteers encamped and drilled here. "It was on this field,"
wrote a chronicler of the event, "that the Brigade by a constant attention
to discipline and tactics acquired so perfect a knowledge of that part of the
military art which relates to evolutions, and the duties of a camp, that it
was considered by experienced officers to have had no superior in the service." [15] The most beautiful tract of the four which Bidermann acquired in
1837, it is no wonder that he found here the ideal site for his future home.

The first structure to be completed was the farmhouse, so carefully
planned by Bidermann while in Paris. It was ready for Evelina and Antoine
(Figs. 6, 7) on their return. Located on the valley floor of Clenny Run, it
was a roomy, three-story house which remained in active service until 1950,
when it was replaced by the present home of Henry Francis du Pont. For
many years it served as a guest house. At the west end of the farmhouse
were the carriage house and stables. As planned, the Bidermanns lived in
this farmhouse throughout 1839 while their new home was being completed.

The spot selected by the Bidermanns for their own residence was the
heavily wooded north slope of the valley through which flowed Clenny Run,
a bit to the east of the farmhouse, at a point half a mile from the Kennett
Pike and half a mile from the county road. The house itself was a handsome structure, departing in many respects from the plans originally drawn
up in Paris by Vergnaud. Designed in the Greek Revival style, it was a
brick and stucco building, three stories high, square, with a flat roof, a
porte-cochere in front (Fig. 8A), and a conservatory-porch in back (Fig.
8B). The porch, with its southern exposure, commanded a fine view down

---

[15] *A Brief Sketch of the Military Operations on the Delaware During the Late War* (Philadelphia, 1820), Winterthur Farms, Winterthur, Delaware. (n.p., privately published, n.d.).

the partly cleared and grass-planted hillside into the valley of Clenny Run and up the opposite wooded hill. The southward extension of the house to the valley floor in 1928 now makes it difficult to imagine this main feature of the original house. The additions of 1884, 1902, and 1928 engulfed most of the original building. Some of it is incorporated into the present structure, as for instance at the Empire Parlor, the Chinese Parlor, and the present Franklin Room; fragments of the original interior architecture have been made part of the Empire Hall display in the present South Wing. (See the article by Jonathan Fairbanks in this issue—Ed.)

The entrance driveway made a handsome sweep from the bridge over Clenny Run up the wooded slope to the porte-cochere and thence eastward and south through the woods and down the slope past the future location of the swimming pool and along the sunken garden. The grounds around the house were lovely in spring, then as now. "The white clover in front of the house . . . is . . . in full bloom," Evelina wrote her son in May, 1844, "and is so fragrant that it perfumes the house. The dogwoods are still in bloom and the lawn on the hill is encircled by them. They are very beautiful mixed in the young green leaves." Down by the Run was a bathhouse screened by plantings of which Evelina was very proud.

With the completion of the gate house on the Kennett Pike, and the handsome drive to Clenny Run, the visitor's approach to Winterthur was an impressive one. A newspaper description published in 1858 does simple justice to the scene, and is evidence of how little it has changed in a hundred years. "The visitor on approaching it from the southern entrance," it states, "is astonished and delighted at the romantic appearance—first at the beautiful fields, as he wends his way on the serpentine road, next passing through the beautiful forest which is decked in various directions with gravelled walks, until he arrives in the valley where the stupendous tenant house, large barns and out buildings attract his attention, surrounded with timber. A short distance to the east on the summit of the hill, also stands the splendid mansion of the proprietor, it is also enclosed with huge oaks and other trees, overlooking the valley and other points . . . . Indeed, we presume, there is not to be found in the country, a more charming and lovely spot." [16]

The first Winterthur garden was a worthy beginning for later horticultural developments. There was a kitchen garden, a small conservatory, beds of flowers around the house, and a sunken garden with a greenhouse just below it. A crab-apple tree planted near this garden by Bidermann, a tulip poplar and two hemlocks that stood just south of the house at this time have been carefully protected through the years and are still standing. (See the article by C. Gordon Tyrrell in this issue—Ed.) Evelina took an active interest in the garden. In the spring of 1844 she wrote her son in Paris, "I have dahlias planted and in bud. The roses and pinks are also just opening, the strawberries shaping . . ." The Bidermanns kept a gardener who lived on the place in his own house which had its own garden near by. The coachman gave occasional help, attending the flower pots near the house and moving the plants in and out of the greenhouse.

Bidermann's second vocation, after 1839, was that of a gentleman farmer, and it was obviously his intention to develop a model agricultural

---

[16] "Winterthur," *The Delaware Republican,* January 7, 1858.

establishment. It was a happy decision, extending a serious avocation of all the du Pont powder-makers on the Brandywine, and inaugurating a Winterthur specialty that was to continue for a hundred years. The farming tradition went back at least as far as Bois des Fossés in France, which Pierre Samuel purchased in 1774 and which his wife, his two sons, and his daughter-in-law Sophie each took turns managing between 1785 and 1799. The tradition was continued at Good Stay, at Bergen Point, New Jersey, with its twenty acres of farmland. On the Brandywine, between 1810 and 1818, Eleuthère Irénée purchased 475 acres of land, and leased 288 more for sheep grazing and grass fodder.[17] Indeed it is quite likely that Bidermann's decision to farm was influenced by the example set by Eleuthère Irénée. The latter, though a manufacturer, was always strongly interested in farming, sheep raising, and tree culture. In Paris, he had studied botany at the Jardin des Plantes; in Delaware, he collected the seeds of many native American trees—including nine varieties of oaks— and sent them to Andre Michaux in France. In 1808 he had become a member of the Philadelphia Society for Promoting Agriculture; he and Victor were members of the Agricultural Society of the County of New Castle when it was incorporated in 1818; its successor, the Agricultural Society of New Castle County, incorporated in 1836, included Henry, Charles I., Alexis, Victor, Eleuthère Irénée II, and Bidermann.[18]

Bidermann's farm was on rich land. A local newspaper described it as "one of the most productive . . . in our State," and having "soil which cannot be exceeded anywhere in point of productiveness."[19] "Everything here grows wonderfully," Evelina wrote her son in 1844. "You would be surprised to see the young orchard and the corn in it . . . We will have peaches in our garden this year and an abundance of strawberries . . . We also have green peas. Yesterday we had 92 hills of sweet potatoes planted. We bid fair also to have a fine crop of turkeys. We have just hatched 18 which is a fair beginning. The ducks are also coming on well, the chickens not so well."[20]

During Bidermann's management, the farm record book distinguished between the Lower Farm and the Winterthur Farm, areas corresponding roughly to the former Martin Farm and Clenny Farm. The Lower Farm was divided into seven fields of a little over 20 acres each. It included a farmhouse, a large dairy of about twenty cows, an orchard of about ten acres, a smaller tenant house and a garden. The Winterthur Farm, containing both arable land and woodland, was divided into nine fields of nearly fifteen acres each. On this farm were located the gate house, dwelling house, carriage house, horse stables, ice houses, the original farmhouse, barn (still standing), a water wheel and pumps to fill the reservoir, an orchard, garden, and a small dairy. In all, there were some five tenant dwellings on the estate occupied by persons variously employed.

Bidermann proved to be as shrewd and business-like in his farming as he had been in his management of the Du Pont Company. At his death, his

[17] ROY M. BOATMAN, "The Agricultural Establishment at Eleutherian Mills, 1802-1834" (unpublished report, Hagley Museum, 1961), p. 1-5.
[18] BOATMAN, p. 41.
[19] "Winterthur," The Delaware Republican, January 7, 1858.
[20] Evelina Bidermann to J. I. Bidermann, May 19, 1844, Bidermann Letters (microfilm 55.6), EMHL.

VUE de la VILLE de WINTERTHUR.

Fig. 9 Winterthur, Switzerland, c. 1800, *colored etching by Johann Jakob Bidermann.*
Coll. Jürg Schoellhorn (Photo. Kunstverein, Winterthur).

farm was thought of as "remarkable for order and good culture."[21] The 1858 description of Winterthur noted that Bidermann "has not only devoted his time to the improvement of the soil . . . but in the laying out of the beautiful walks, in building of neat fences, clearing the underbrush from the timber, and in the erection of large and capacious barns which have all the modern improvements arranged in a manner unsurpassed for comfort and convenience." Listing recent improvements, it referred to two large additions made to the Winterthur Farm barn, and "many other improvements introduced for preparing or cooking food for cattle and other stock. His steaming apparatus is most complete, and the stalls are furnished in a superior manner, making them almost equal to dwelling houses for comfort. A large reservoir has been constructed, which furnishes the barn as well as the dwelling with water, and every other improvement almost which can be suggested for utility and convenience." His superintendent for the Winterthur Farm was described as "one of the most skilful and experienced agriculturalists in our state." Certainly the voluminous and detailed farm records are a model of administrative efficiency.

Bidermann was meticulous about soil improvement, drainage, and quality of livestock. The program for the rotation of crops was "corn, oats,

---

[21] *Delaware State Journal and Statesman,* July 11, 1865.

wheat, and six years of grass." The fields were fertilized at a ratio of thirty bushels an acre with the lime of oyster shells burned on the place. Steady progress was made in draining swamp land. The livestock included a large herd of Devon cattle (a particularly valuable bull was named William Tell), pigs, and a good stable of horses. Evelina described the favorite saddle horse, Henry Clay, as "handsome, sleek, and spirited."

It is not certain just when the Bidermanns decided to call their new home "Winterthur," but the name does appear at the head of a letter which Antoine wrote his son in July, 1842. It was natural to name the Delaware estate after the town of Winterthur (Fig. 9) located fifteen miles from Zurich in northeast Switzerland, for this ancient city, established as a fortress by the Romans in 294 A.D., and given its town charter by Rudolf of Hapsburg in 1264, was rich in associations for Bidermann. From 1790 until 1804 he had spent a happy childhood and commenced his education there. He revisited it as often as he could, for after his father's death in 1817 it was his mother's home until her death in 1842, and we know that he went to see her there in 1828 and 1838. Winterthur was, moreover, the birthplace of his father and of his father's father, and, indeed, the Bidermann connection with Winterthur goes back to the years when the present Zurich Canton was the Winterthur Canton. An early ancestor of the family, Arnold Bidermann, Graf von Goldenberg, lived there and served as deputy of the Helvetian cantons in the service of Charles de Hardy, Duke of Burgundy. Several Bidermann daughters married counts of Kyburg of the House of Hapsburg whose castle was four miles south of the town.[22] "Winterthur," like "Nemours," "Montchanin," and "Granogue" testifies to the Continental origin of the landowners of the lower Brandywine Valley.

Bidermann prospered as a farmer, breeder, investor, and a Du Pont Company stockholder. His benefactions included a gift of $1,000, a magic lantern, and agricultural books to the Center Grove public school in his neighborhood, and gifts to Christ Church Christiana Hundred, of which he and Evelina were members. In politics, he stood with Henry du Pont as a staunch Henry Clay Whig, and later, a loyal advocate of the Union cause. Like so many of the du Ponts, Bidermann was a hard-working man, and much of the success of the Winterthur farms was due to the long, hard hours of work that he put into them. He often got up at five in the morning to oversee the estate chores.

Antoine, however, had never been really robust; visits to Sulphur Springs, New York, helped him only a little, and in the late fifties he developed a serious illness. In 1858, old age and declining health forced him to put his farm on shares. His eyesight, too, was failing. When Evelina died on March 19, 1863, after a severe illness of three months, he was seventy-four years old and there was little to keep him at Winterthur: he was alone in the big house, he had no blood relatives to keep him in America, and his son was firmly settled in France. It is small wonder, therefore, that he decided to leave Winterthur and join his son's family. He appointed Charles I. du Pont, Jr., and Henry du Pont as his administrators, and wrote out for them detailed instructions as to renting or selling his

---

[22] "Winterthur" (tourist leaflet, Winterthur, Switzerland, Geschwister Ziegler & Co., n.d.), Mme George S. Hueber, MS memorandum dated April, 1961, Winterthur Memorial Library.

Fig. 11
Henry du Pont, *engraving*
by J. J. Cade, New York, of oil
portrait by unknown artist. Coll.
Eleutherian Mills Historical Library.

Fig. 10 James Irénée Bidermann,
photograph in Du Pont de Nemours,
1800-1900, Album, *Vol. I, #78,*
Eleutherian Mills Historical Library.

properties together or separately.[23] Antoine Bidermann died in Paris on June 8, 1865. The obituary in the *Delaware State Journal and Statesman* described him justly as a man of "sound judgment, a strong and cultivated intellect, untiring energy, and unbending integrity."

When, in 1863, Bidermann announced his intention of returning to France and selling Winterthur, there was naturally some thought that a member of the du Pont family might purchase it. Admiral Samuel Francis du Pont was one who thought seriously of this. He was on the point of retirement from active duty in the navy, and both he and his wife feared the constant threat to their home Louviers from the frequent explosions of the Hagley powder mills across the Brandywine. "Do you know," he wrote his wife in June, 1863, "I have thought more than once of our taking Winterthur and closing our days there . . . I don't think I would find it lonesome, and it would be sure to fix my life, because I never would leave you alone there as I have too much by far at our own dear home." Three weeks later he wrote again, "I shall take care not to say a word about Winterthur—though the more I think of it, the more I incline to it, though my heart would bleed a little at giving up our home."[24] The Admiral, however, died in 1865 before he could act on the purchase. Winterthur was not sold before Bidermann left Delaware, nor before he died in France, but it may have been rented. On Antoine's death, Winterthur passed to his son.

[23] J. A. Bidermann to C. I. du Pont, Jr., August 1, 1863, Bidermann Letter Book, (microfilm 55.6), EMHL.

[24] S. F. du Pont to wife, June 5, 28, 1863, The Henry Francis du Pont Winterthur MSS Collection, EMHL.

The second owner of Winterthur, James Irénée Bidermann (Fig. 10), had been brought up on the Brandywine in the widening circle of du Pont grandparents, uncles, and aunts and had received a solid American education. In 1829 he went off to The New Haven Gymnasium, a boy's boarding school in New Haven, Connecticut, in the company of his young uncle, Alexis I. du Pont who was a son of Eleuthère Irénée du Pont, and only one year and seven months older than he. Upon graduation, he continued, with Alexis, to the University of Pennsylvania and graduated from there. He returned to France with his parents in 1837, was admitted to the École Polytechnique, and decided to remain in France when his parents returned to Delaware. After another visit home, he returned to France in 1842 and became a railroad engineer.[25] Two years later he married Gabrielle Camille Begue, addressed as "Camille" by her relatives, and the couple made their home in France, living first at Cherbourg and later at Brienon L'Archeveque (Yonne). Camille visited her husband's family and relatives in 1844, and surviving correspondence between her and several members of the du Pont family testify to a warm and continuing friendship. Evelina was especially fond of Camille, and apparently knew her father and sisters, yet she and Antoine found it almost impossible to accept the son's decision to remain in France.

On June 1, 1866, Henry du Pont mailed to James I. Bidermann a purchase offer for Winterthur, and on July 25 Bidermann agreed to his uncle's offer. "I need not mention," he added in his letter of acceptance, "that I am satisfied to think that the Winterthur Estate shall remain in the family. I am sure now that all my father's works will be respected and continued if possible." The deed of sale was signed in Paris on February 4, 1867, witnessed by the American Consul, and delivered to Henry in March.

Henry du Pont (Fig. 11) had at least three good motives in purchasing Winterthur and thus becoming its third owner. The factor of sentiment certainly weighed heavily with him: even though he had no immediate, personal need of Winterthur, being now comfortably settled at Eleutherian Mills, nevertheless he could not see the home of his sister and of a brother-in-law whom he had known intimately all his life pass out of the family. Furthermore, he had even helped his brother-in-law to build Winterthur during 1838-39. A second motive was equally strong: Henry's oldest son, Henry Algernon, was in 1867 in the midst of an active military career with the U. S. Army and was still unmarried, but he would be returning to civilian life in a few years and Winterthur would make an ideal home for him. In the third place, Henry du Pont, like his father and grandfather before him, was passionately interested in farm land. By 1866, there were twenty parcels of land amounting to 1,476 acres carried on the company books[26], and much of this had been acquired by him. His personal estate, of which Winterthur was now a part, would soon consist of 2,000 acres, making him, reputedly, the biggest landowner in Delaware.[27] He spent thousands of dollars in improving and enriching his farmland, much of it in experimental undertakings.[28] His additions to Winterthur increased its size from the 445 acres he originally purchased to 1,135 acres (Fig. 5) through

[25] Preface, Bidermann Letters (microfilm 55.6), EMHL.
[26] BOATMAN, p. 11.
[27] Ibid., p. 41.
[28] Daily Republican, August 8, 1889.

eleven separate purchases. In 1861, Henry du Pont had been appointed Major-General, commanding Delaware's volunteers, and may indeed have done as much as anybody to keep the State on the Union side. Thereafter everyone knew him as "The General."

The General probably never lived at Winterthur, but he surely kept a close and appreciative eye on it. As the fourth head of the Du Pont Company, serving from 1850 until his death in 1889 for what was to be the longest term in the company's history, his closest attention was given to the mills on the Brandywine. However, we know that Henry du Pont greatly enjoyed driving from Eleutherian Mills out over his extensive estate in his familiar buggy, his greyhounds accompanying him, "looking at his crops and his stock, and picking out points for improvement in soil and plant, in fence and building."[29] He doubtless rented the residence on Clenny Run to acquaintances from time to time between 1867 and 1874; in 1876 he welcomed his son to Winterthur, and apparently kept a restraining hand on the latter's considerable alterations to the house. His flaming red beard, his black, stovepipe hat, and his Henry Clay cigar were well-known throughout the countryside, and his aggressive, spartan personality lent to Winterthur through these years a vital, brisk, austerity.

Henry A. du Pont, the fourth owner of Winterthur, was a year old when the Bidermanns returned from France and began their residence on Clenny Run. He grew up knowing his Aunt Evelina and Uncle Antoine as neighbors living close by his home at Eleutherian Mills. He must have accompanied his parents to Winterthur on many a family visit during the years when he was a student at Dr. Lyon's School at West Haverford, later at the University of Pennsylvania, and at West Point. He was campaigning in Virginia as an artillery officer with the Union army when Bidermann decided to return to France in 1863, and was in command at Camp Williams, Virginia, when his father acquired the Bidermann estate in 1867 and notified him that it would be waiting for him when he chose to leave the Army for civilian life. During his honeymoon trip to France in 1874-75, he frequently visited members of the Bidermann family. The Colonel lived at Winterthur from 1875 to 1926, inheriting the estate from his father in 1889. Under its second resident owner, Winterthur gained new distinction: not only were the residence, the gardens, the farm and the over-all estate enlarged, but the home reflected the many-sided interests and the active hospitality of an active officer of the Du Pont Company, a railroad executive, a United States Senator, a family archivist, and in many ways the social head of the numerous du Pont family in its third generation.

Henry A. du Pont's career in the United States Army was a notable one.[30] Fort Sumter had just been fired on when he was graduated from West Point at the head of his class with a second lieutenant's commission in the Corps of Engineers. He won steady promotion. First assigned to duty with the Fifth Pennsylvania Volunteers in the defense of Washington, D. C., he was almost immediately promoted to first lieutenant, and in 1864 was advanced to captain in command of Light Battery B, Fifth Regiment of U. S. Artillery; in the spring of 1864 he became chief of artillery, Army

[29] *Ibid.*
[30] HENRY A. DU PONT, *A Genealogical-Biographical History of the du Pont Family* (n.p., National Americana Society, 1923), pp. 29-30.

Fig. 12
Colonel Henry A. du Pont
in Dress Uniform *(63.826),*
Winterthur Museum.

of West Virginia. From July 1863, he saw service in the field, first in Pennsylvania, then in Maryland, Virginia, and West Virginia. On May 15, 1864, he fought in the battle of Newmarket in Sigel's campaign in the Valley of Virginia, and subsequently in the battles of Piedmont and Lynchburg. On September 19 he was made brevet major for "gallant and meritorious conduct at the Battles of Winchester and Fisher's Hill, Virginia"; and on October 19, was brevetted lieutenant colonel for "distinguished service at the Battle of Cedar Creek." Years later, in 1898, he was awarded the Congressional Medal of Honor for his part in this battle, the citation being for "most distinguished gallantry and voluntary exposure to the enemy's fire at a critical moment."

After the War, Colonel du Pont continued in service with his artillery regiment in Maryland and Virginia, being assigned tours of duty during 1866-67 as commander of Fort Munroe and Camp Williams in Virginia; and during 1868-72 as commander of Sedgwick Barracks in Washington, D. C., and Fort Adams at Newport, Rhode Island (Fig. 12). He enjoyed the military profession, and his close associates included such Army leaders as General-in-Chief William T. Sherman, Generals James H. Wilson, John Schofield, Emory Upton, Winfield Scott Hancock, and others, as well as Congressman, later President, James A. Garfield. His war experience qualified him for a key role on an Army board of officers appointed to serve from January, 1873, until September, 1874, to assimilate Upton's infantry tactics to the other arms, resulting in the revision of two U. S. War Department manuals, *Cavalry Tactics, U. S. Army, Assimilated to Tactics of*

Fig. 13 Winterthur House, 1885-1902, Garden Front, *Winterthur Museum.*

Infantry and Artillery, and *Artillery Tactics, U. S. Army, Assimilated to the Tactics of Infantry and Cavalry,* published by D. Appleton in 1874 and 1875 respectively. Incidentally, the essentials of the system worked out by du Pont and his fellow officers continue to dominate American tactics.[31]

Civilian associations, however, were now becoming determinative. The Colonel's engagement to Mary Pauline Foster of New York was announced in September, 1873, and on completion of the two Army manuals which required his presence at West Point, he was married in July, 1874. After a year of travel and residence in Europe, Colonel du Pont formally resigned from the Army in March, 1875. That October, he and his wife took up their residence at Winterthur.

"The Colonel," as Henry A. du Pont was known, remodeled and enlarged the Winterthur residence on three different occasions. The first was in 1874, a few weeks after his wedding and a month or so before sailing to Europe on his honeymoon. He had come to Winterthur with his young bride, and discussed the changes he wished made with Theophilus P. Chandler, a Philadelphia architect who was the Colonel's brother-in-law. Chandler made a sketch of the proposed alterations which Mary Pauline thought "a lovely addition," and in a letter that December reviewed all the proposals, including the ones that "The General" had disapproved. One feature which would have considerably changed the exterior—to rebuild the conservatory on the south side so as to include a new library between it and the house—was apparently not realized. Internal improvements mentioned by Chandler included the addition of a large arch to the first floor hall, relocation of the fireplace, a new dumb waiter, a new bathroom on the second floor, and stairs to the roof on the third floor.[32]

---

[31] Stephen E. Ambrose to the author, October 25, 1963, letter in possession of the author.
[32] Letter from T. P. Chandler to H. A. du Pont, December 13, 1874, The Henry Francis du Pont Winterthur MSS Collection, EMHL.

Fig. 14 Winterthur House, 1902-1928, from Northeast, *Winterthur Museum.*

The second remodeling took place in 1884. The original flat roof was replaced by a steep slate roof and raised to include an attic; dormer windows and tall brick chimneys were added (Fig. 13). The change was dramatic. When a friend heard about it, she wrote to the Colonel's wife, "I don't believe I shall recognize your much changed house with its gables, and tiles, and turrets. It must look quite a castle."

The third remodeling, and the most extensive one, was carried out during 1902-1903 (Fig. 14). On the north, an entire new front was built, one room deep, with a new porte-cochere and front door, and behind it a large new entrance stairhall; to the east, a new three-story wing was built containing, from basement up, a squash court, billiard room, and library; on the west was added, over the old wine cellar, a new first-floor drawing room decorated with an Italian ceiling and walls of red damask which was later to become the Marlboro Room. The rest of the entrance floor was not much changed. The Colonel's office and the parlor were made into one room, now the Empire Parlor, and furnished with Louis XVI furniture, and the old dining room was enlarged by combining it with the little sitting room in the area now occupied by the Chinese Parlor. Heavy Spanish tiles replaced the slate on the roof, new terra cotta cornices took the place of the old wooden cornices, and dormers in the style known as Francis I were installed in approximately the position of the old simple dormers. Meanwhile, nearly all the original walls had to be taken down and rebuilt as they were not strong enough to support the new roof.[33] The new Winterthur home was both stylish and distinguished.

[33] HENRY FRANCIS DU PONT, "The Building of Winterthur Museum," *Winterthur Illustrated,* (Winterthur, Delaware: The Henry Francis du Pont Winterthur Museum, 1963), p. 7; H. A. du Pont to Pauline du Pont, August 17, 20, 1902, The Henry Francis du Pont Winterthur MSS Collection, EMHL.

The Colonel loved Winterthur's gardens and grounds. It was with great relief that he could report to his wife, during the remodeling of the house in 1902, that it would be possible to save the climbing euonymous which still thrives along the outside west wall of the Winterthur Museum. During the same summer, when a big chestnut tree in the field near the gatehouse was struck by lightning, he wrote, "I shall feel terribly if this injury should kill the poor old tree, one of the few remaining relics of the primeval forest." The Colonel did much to extend and develop both gardens and grounds, and in this he had, from 1902 onwards, the enthusiastic and increasingly knowledgeable collaboration of his son Henry Francis. Five developments which father and son carried out during the next eighteen years became increasingly important: the new greenhouses, the new sunken garden, the March Bank, the Pinetum, and the Azalea Woods.

The year 1902 saw the extensive remodeling not only of the house, but the garden area. The two greenhouses to the southeast of the residence, of which one went back to Bidermann's day, were salvaged and three new ones were built behind the coachhouse, with a new potting shed. A new sunken garden and terraced garden in front of the long pit below the three greenhouses were also built. The old sunken garden, which was Henry Francis's great-aunt Evelina du Pont Bidermann's rose garden, and which his mother took care of and enjoyed all her life, was redesigned, enlarged, and built with four terraces. The lower one remained the rose garden; a water lily pool and three arbors of wisteria were located on the next terrace, with the third one much as it is now. An arbor-covered wall fountain set between two garden houses, and a small swimming pool were where the swimming pool is now. At the same time, the March Bank of spring flowers was begun along the path just north of the porte-cochere. Henry Francis began by naturalizing early spring bulbs there, and above them the daffodils which still bloom every year.

In 1914, after the beginning of the war, father and son were in England for several weeks and visited many beautiful country homes. On his return home, and with these English examples in mind, the Colonel laid out the Pinetum with over fifty species and varieties of trees which have remained ever since almost exactly as they were planted. At the same time two tennis courts were built at the base of the small Pinetum hill. In 1920, Henry Francis established the Azalea Woods with a nucleus of Kurume azaleas which he had purchased in 1917 and carefully cultivated, and some Torch azaleas which had been sent him in 1919 from the Arnold Arboretum. Meanwhile the lawns around the house had been extended, beyond them the virgin growth had been carefully preserved with new plantings of trees and shrubs added, and in 1925 several new roads and paths through the grounds were opened up. In 1924, four more greenhouses and the cold frames were added, and in 1926 the fig house, vegetable house, and connecting house. Happily, all of these additions to the Winterthur gardens and grounds are still enjoyed today.

The Colonel carried on the tradition of scientific farming established by his grandfather and continued by his father. It was an interest shared by his father-in-law and brother-in-law, Herman Ten Eyck Foster in New York and A. Lentilhon Foster in Christiana Hundred. The Colonel's obituary in the *Wilmington Morning News* accurately notes that "he had a deep interest in every phase of farming, and a broad understanding of, and sympathy with, agricultural problems." With his retirement from the railroad connection in 1899, he turned more and more to the development of the Winterthur Farms.

One of the Colonel's most persistent interests was the acquisition of the lands adjoining Winterthur so as to extend its boundaries. In nineteen of the forty years between 1885 and 1925, he made twenty-five purchases to add 900 acres to the Winterthur holdings, filling out this handsome enclave between the Kennett Pike, Kirk Road, the Company's holdings, and the Brandywine (Fig. 5). In 1918 the Farm comprised about 1,446 acres of cleared land, of which some 941 were tillable, and 430 acres of woodland. A second important interest was the development of a Holstein herd. When Bidermann's Devon cattle were replaced by purebred Holsteins is not clear, but the first purebred Holstein to carry the Winterthur name, Belle of Winterthur, was born in 1893. The Colonel joined the Holstein-Friesian Association of America in 1895. His political activities, however, took an increasing amount of his time and interest, and by 1914 the quality of the herd had declined. His most important action in promoting the Winterthur Farm was his decision to let his son Henry Francis take over its management in 1914. The resulting expansion in dairy, breeding, and crop activities is summarized below.

Very soon after the end of the Civil War, the Colonel's father and Lammot du Pont urged him to leave the Army and join the Company. He was at first unwilling to do this, being devoted to his military profession. After his marriage in 1874, however, he realized what a hardship it would be to his wife to have no settled home, and so resigned from the Army and in 1878 became a Company partner.[34] He served as sales manager (being well posted on military and naval needs) and took charge of traffic arrangements and negotiations with the railroads at a time when the practice of rebates and drawbacks made this a delicate and important mission. On his father's death in 1889, the Colonel was, by seniority, entitled to succeed him as senior partner of the Company, but it was decided that leadership responsibility should go to a practical powder-maker, and so his first cousin Eugene was chosen. In 1899 he successfully urged termination of the partnership begun in 1837, and the incorporation of the Company, and became, in this year, one of the three newly-created vice-presidents. On the death of Eugene in 1902, the Colonel was asked to take the presidency and declined, giving his support to the sale of the Company to Alfred I. and his two cousins, Pierre S. and T. Coleman.[35] All in all, his services to the Company were substantial.

A special chapter of Winterthur history concerns the fortunes of the Wilmington and Northern Railroad.[36] It was originally chartered in 1861 as the Wilmington and Brandywine Railroad to run from the Philadelphia, Wilmington and Baltimore Railroad near Old Swedes Church to Chadds

[34] B. G. DU PONT, Interview with Henry A. du Pont, "Notes for History," pp. 822-23, Longwood MSS, EMHL.

[35] DUTTON, pp. 124, 164, 170; JOHN K. WINKLER, *The Du Pont Dynasty,* (New York: Reynal and Hitchcock, 1935), p. 148.

[36] WILMINGTON & READING RAILROAD, *From Coal to Tide* (Wilmington, Delaware: Jenkins and Atkinson, 1870); GEORGE ROMMEL, PAUL R. EPPLER, "History of the Wilmington and Northern Railroad," MSS, Wilmington Institute Free Library.

Fig. 15
Anne de Montchanin *(61.1745),*
oil portrait by unknown artist,
Winterthur Museum.

Ford Junction as part of a plan to move anthracite coal more directly from the Pennsylvania mines to factories at and near Wilmington. In 1865 it was renamed the Delaware and Pennsylvania State Line Railway, and the following year was consolidated with the Berks and Chester Railroad to become the Wilmington and Reading Railway Company. The right-of-way across Winterthur was secured some time between 1861 and 1869, and the first track was laid in 1869; in January, 1870, the road opened for freight and regular passenger trains between Wilmington and Coatesville, and in 1874 between Wilmington and Reading. In January, 1877, the name of the line was changed to the Wilmington and Northern Railroad.

In 1878, the Colonel became a director of the Wilmington and Northern, and the following year became its president and general manager. He thereupon divided his time between the powder company and the railroad, usually going to the Company office in the morning and the railroad office in the afternoon. Under his proficient direction, the Wilmington and Northern was reorganized and well managed—for example, it became the first railway in the region to try out electric headlights—and it was of great value to the Company in moving powder. A spur from Montchanin to the powder works was used as late as 1917. Considerable traffic developed on the line in the 'nineties; in addition to the freight trains, there were three passenger trains each day going both ways. The Colonel's administration may be best remembered today for the place names he gave to four of the stations built nearby. The Montchanin Station (orginally known as Du Pont Station) was named after the Colonel's great-great-grandmother Anne Alexandrine de Montchanin (Fig. 15), mother of Pierre Samuel du Pont de Nemours, and the person most responsible for guiding him into a career of scholarship. The station names Granogue and Guyencourt (formerly Center Station) were taken from places in France associated with the family. Cossart, just over the Pennsylvania line, was named after Marie Cossart who married Abraham du Pont; the two were

Colonel du Pont's great-great-great-great-great grandparents. The stop for Winterthur was at first located where Adams Dam Road crossed the track, but in the mid eighteen-nineties the present Winterthur Station was built on the estate and in it was established a fourth class (after 1951 a third class) U. S. post office. In 1898, the line was taken over by the Philadelphia and Reading Railway, of which the Colonel served as a director until 1906.

In addition to his active interests in the family company, the Wilmington and Northern Railway, and the Winterthur Farm, the Colonel became actively involved in state and national politics. During the mid-nineties, the Republican party in Delaware was badly split and in turmoil. The Colonel was elected by the regulars to lead the party and to run for the U. S. Senate. In the election of 1895, his supporters claimed that he was elected, but the vote was not only tied but contested, and in the end the Colonel was not seated. Determined to do his duty, he attended State conventions and other political gatherings, presenting a picture of what his friends later recalled as a "patient, unfaltering, adamant, heroic figure." [37] In 1906, he was elected to the U. S. Senate by the Delaware State legislature, and took his seat in December. In 1911, receiving the entire Republican vote of the legislature, he was reelected for a term ending in March, 1917. From 1911 to 1913 he was chairman of the Senate Military Affairs Committee at a crucial time, when the army was being reorganized on the eve of World War I. In 1897, President McKinley offered him the appointment of Minister to Russia, which he declined; in 1918 and 1920, he continued to be active in Delaware state politics.

A fourth interest of the Colonel made Winterthur, by 1900, the chief depository of du Pont family papers and the home of the recognized family historian. It was doubtless Admiral du Pont's widow, Sophie M. du Pont, herself a skillful family archivist, who first communicated to Henry A. the satisfaction and excitement of gathering materials bearing on the history of the family, and guided him in his first efforts. As early as 1856, when he was only 18, he was already digging into family records in the Delaware-New Jersey-Pennsylvania area.[38] During his sojourn in Europe during 1874-1875, with the help of trained assistants, he systematically combed through five centuries of French records in provincial as well as Parisian archives to locate and make copies of relevant documents. The Admiral's widow soon decided that her nephew should assume responsibility for the family archives after her death. They worked closely together during the last two years of her life, and in 1888 the rich materials which had accumulated at Louviers passed in a block to Winterthur. The Colonel's transcripts from foreign archives and his extensive correspondence with searchers, librarians, and scholars attest his thoroughness and scholarly standards. Out of his own and the family records, he published three volumes: *The Campaign of 1864 in the Valley of Virginia and the Expedition to Lynchburg* (New York, 1925), *The Early Generations of the du Pont and Allied Families* (New York, 1923), and *Rear-Admiral Samuel Francis du Pont, A Biography* (New York, 1926). Meanwhile he was assembling materials for a memoir of Pierre Samuel du Pont de Nemours.

[37] *Wilmington Morning News,* January 1, 1927.
[38] CHARLES W. DAVID, "The Longwood Library," *Papers of the Bibliographical Society of America*, Vol. 51, 3rd Quarterly, 1957.

Fig. 16
Henry A. du Pont in 1906
(64.1190), oil portrait
by Ellen Emmet,
Winterthur Museum.

When his son authorized a report and inventory of the Colonel's published and manuscript holdings in 1957 and 1959, it was estimated that these contained over 160,000 manuscript items and 5,274 imprints. Almost all of this collection, which contained some invaluable papers of both family, national, and general interest, was given to the Longwood Library (now the Eleutherian Mills Historical Library) and is there catalogued as the Henry Francis du Pont Winterthur Collections, forming a substantial part of what is undoubtedly one of the most remarkable collections of family records in this country. It is possible, as one scholar has suggested, that the Colonel might well have made a significant contribution to American letters had not other activities claimed him. "One is strongly tempted to infer," writes the former Director of the Longwood Library, "that heavy military, political, and business demands of his time robbed us of an outstanding academic figure, for genealogical research as refined as his indisputably requires the highest degree of intellectual versatility and discipline."[39]

The portrait of the Colonel painted by Ellen Emmet in 1906 (Fig. 16) which hangs in the Museum's Memorial Library suggests the West Point graduate, the scholar, and the cultivated man of the world. During the fifty years that he lived there, Winterthur knew its special joys and sorrows. The Colonel's daughter, Louise Evelina, was born in 1877, and his son, Henry Francis in 1880. There were five other children who died in infancy. The daughter's debut brought a host of friends and acquaintances

---

[39] *Ibid.*

to the home in 1897, as did her marriage here to Francis Boardman Crowninshield in 1900. Sorrow came in the fall of 1902 with the death of the Colonel's wife. It must have been a great pleasure to the Colonel when in 1923 his daughter and her husband made their residence at Eleutherian Mills close by. After his final term in the U. S. Senate was concluded in 1917, he gave himself to the joys and responsibilities of looking after his estate, dying suddenly of heart failure on the last day of 1926 at the age of eighty-eight.

When Henry Francis du Pont inherited Winterthur in 1926, he was already well launched on the three life interests in which he has won so much distinction. He had been giving thoughtful attention to gardening and horticulture since 1902; he had taken over management of his father's farm and laid the foundation of the Winterthur herd in 1914; and American antiques had claimed his serious attention since 1924. Mr. du Pont has continued his active participation in each of these three fields and in each he has brought lustre to Winterthur. Behind each of these major accomplishments, and behind each minor day-to-day decision necessary to promote them, are evident the special traits that mark his success: clear cut purpose, meticulous attention to details, use of expert advice, readiness to experiment, superb judgment and instantaneous decision, and above all, a passionate search for not only excellence but perfection.

Henry Francis du Pont had taken an active part in developing the Winterthur garden and grounds from the time of his graduation from Harvard. The March Bank of spring flowers, and the Azalea Woods were his particular early creations. After the Colonel's death he referred to himself as Winterthur's head gardener, and as such he worked hard to accomplish some outstanding results. As always, he proceeded in accordance with a plan, and his plan called for naturalized woodland plantings carefully arranged to take advantage of every vista, and to constitute, at all times, harmonies of color in which background masses created a setting for spring blooms. Tanbark walks and green turf paths gave the visitor ready access to what became, by 1960, a meticulously planned garden of forty acres.

Between 1927 and 1930 there were important developments in the Pinetum area. Here Henry Francis laid out paths through the conifers, planted crab-apple trees, white azaleas, and other shrubs, and placed at the end of a path the lovely white garden gate from Latimeria. Beyond the Pinetum, in 1928, he constructed an eighty-acre, ten-hole golf course with the same extra set of tees. Designed by the firm of Emmet and Tull, it had the reputation of being one of the largest such courses in the country. Then, beginning across the lawn from the first tee, he also planned and planted the Chaenomeles Path with steps here and there to the armillary Sundial Garden below a nine-foot-wide grass walk with ample space on both sides for specimen chaenomeles. With the background of the conifers in mid-April, these blooming shrubs of rose, pale pink, white, deep red and salmon are one of the best displays at Winterthur. The next year he laid out a croquet court near the tennis courts by the Pinetum and screened these with box. Meanwhile, a strong interest in primulas led him to establish a primula quarry near what today is the Meadow Parking Lot, while at the same time he added charm to the Peony Garden by erecting there several garden ornaments.

Between 1935 and 1951, further significant additions were made to the Azalea Woods, the Peony Garden, and the Pinetum area. Mr. du Pont's interest in azaleas and rhododendrons led him to secure many choice specimens from nurseries in various parts of the country and then carefully to cultivate them at Winterthur, starting them in the cutting garden nursery and then transferring them to the Azalea Woods. The latter, located on a wooded hill overlooking the Museum, grew steadily in importance. In 1946 the area received its present general plan, and today includes more than 235 species and varieties, with the total number of plants well into the thousands.[40] In the meantime, the Peony Garden was enriched by a small group of Japanese tree peonies and by hybrids from the gardens of Professor A. P. Saunders and renamed the Saunders Peony Garden. Today this garden contains almost two hundred individual plants of the Saunders hybrids. Finally, Oak Hill, which overlooks the residence and the valley on the east, was developed according to a plan that included planting young oaks, several varieties of dogwood, and azaleas.

As in his other two major avocations, Mr. du Pont's gardening has been marked by the judgment of the connoisseur and the zeal of the perfectionist. He was the trusted friend of experts in nurseries, aboretums and horticultural circles who sent him rare plants that had just become known in this country. These were given meticulous care and were then combined with native plantings that came to include almost every forest tree and flower which grows in Delaware. When he found a sport of azalea 'Magnifica' in the garden, he named it 'Winterthur' and carefully cultivated it. Meanwhile, he exercised his keen sense of color harmony to organize his azalea and rhododendron gardens with a masterful eye to color combination, shifting plants about to get the effect he wanted, and ruthlessly removing ones that did not fit. The planning and care of the trees on the estate, in connection with what other members of the du Pont family were doing and had done for four generations, was judged to have made "the neighborhood of Wilmington one of the chief centers of horticulture in the United States." [41] All this combined to make the Winterthur gardens a delight to both the uninformed and the expert.

It was this conscientious exercise of the art and science of gardening that brought Mr. du Pont many of the top honors in this field. He is a vice president of the Horticultural Society of New York (president from 1935 until 1946), a member of the Board of Directors of the New York Botanical Garden, and a life member of the Brooklyn Botanic Garden; chairman of the Horticultural Committee, and a Visitor to the Arnold Arboretum; a member of the Board of Managers of the Fairchild Tropical Garden; a member of the Advisory Council of the Morris Arboretum; chairman of the Advisory Committee of Longwood Gardens; and vice president of the Royal Horticultural Society (Great Britain). He has received the George Robert White Medal of Honor of the Massachusetts Horticultural Society, the Distinguished Service Award of the New York Botanical Garden and of the Horticultural Society of New York, the Special Award of the Horticultural Society of New York, and the two highest

[40] C. Gordon Tyrrell, "Winterthur Gardens," *Rhododendron and Camelia Yearbook, 1963* (London, 1962), pp. 28-34.
[41] Charles S. Sargent, "Notes on North American Trees," *Journal of the Arnold Arboretum,* V (1924), p. 47.

awards given to nonprofessional horticulturists—the Gold Medal of the National Association of Gardeners and the Medal of Honor of the Garden Club of America. Of the former, only six others have been given since the Association was founded in 1911. The press release on the latter included the following statement: "He is conceded by fellow horticulturists to be one of the best, even the best gardener this country has ever produced. Since boyhood he has been interested in gardening. This culminated in the great achievement of his estate, Winterthur, where he established a botanical garden of dramatic beauty. The woodland trees under-planted with a profusion of native wildflowers and rhododendron, acres of dogwood, banks of azaleas, lilies and peonies, iris and other rare specimens from many lands are planted with taste and discrimination, and form one of the world's great gardens. Ever generous in contributing his knowledge and support, his advice is sought by almost every horticultural organization in America and the Royal Horticultural Society of London."

Under the administration of Henry Francis du Pont, the family estate reached its largest extent in acreage, its most numerous population, and its most varied and industrious pattern of activities. Like his great-grandfather Irénée, his grandfather Henry, and his father, Henry Algernon, Henry Francis purchased new land in accordance with a careful plan of rounding out Winterthur's boundaries. Between 1900 and 1922, while his father was still enlarging the estate, he added some 382 acres to Winterthur in his own name (Fig. 5). When he inherited Winterthur in 1926, it totaled about 2,400 acres, extending roughly between the Kennett Pike, Kirk Road, Rockland Road, the Brandywine Creek, Guyencourt Road, Center Meeting Road, and Pyle-Ford Road, and this was to be its greatest extent.

"Winterthur" was the general name for the several parts of a varied, busy estate. Roughly, these parts could be divided into two: the operations associated directly with the residence, and those associated with the Winterthur Farms (Fig. 17). The former included some twelve acres around the residence; the four-acre cutting gardens started by the Colonel with an acre of cold frames, and a two-acre propagating garden for azaleas; the vegetable garden, the greenhouses, the lawns and gardens which eventually comprised some 40 acres, and the golf course of 80 acres. Winterthur Farms included the land under cultivation, the dairy, and the balance of the property. On the estate there were about ninety houses, most of them occupied by individuals and families employed at Winterthur. Though exact figures are not available, it is likely that the population of Winterthur may have come close to 250. With its own railroad station and post office, its own water supply, farm, and shops, it was almost a self-sufficient community.

The farming operation had two main objectives: to supply this considerable community, and particularly Mr. du Pont's table, with meat, fruit, vegetables, and dairy products; and to maintain the Winterthur herd. Apart from the Holstein herd which at one time numbered almost 450 cows, the livestock included some 250 Herefords, 100 hogs, 100 Dorset sheep, 45 horses including some purebred Percherons, and 2,300 poultry—chickens, turkeys, guinea hens, Muscovy ducks, and Mallards. In 1929, the acres planted to feed the livestock included 372 to alfalfa, 90 to ensilage, 80 to wheat, 16 to corn, and 3 to beets. Wheat was the only cash crop, but sales included Holstein bulls, beef cattle, hogs, milk and eggs, a little wool, and some seed corn.

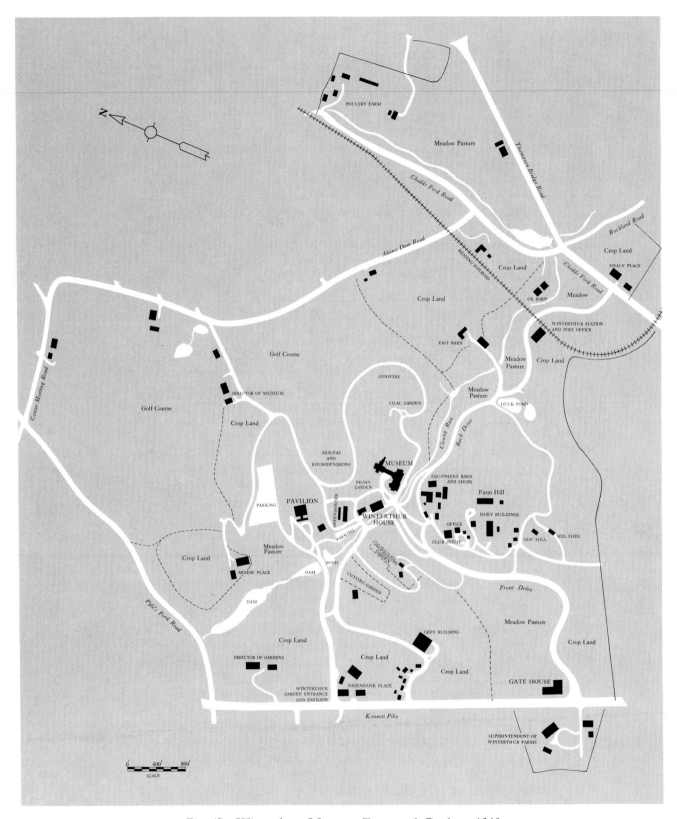

Fig. 17   Winterthur: Museum, Farm, and Gardens, 1960
after a drawing by Leslie Potts, 1963

The tradition of scientific farm management, started at Winterthur by Bidermann, has been vigorously continued by Henry Francis du Pont. Well-equipped blacksmith, carpenter, butcher shops, and a laundry service the entire estate. A central farm office keeps meticulous records, cottages are provided for married employees, and, until recently, a boarding house was maintained for single men, and a club house with a theatre to serve the farm community as a whole. There was a billiard table in the club house, and in the theatre were held concerts by the Farm band, occasional church services, and Sunday School Classes. Just as the milking machines replaced hand milking, so tractors replaced horses as improvement followed improvement. The first cluster of farm buildings was on the side of "Farm Hill" to the south of the run below the residence; in 1918, Henry Francis created a new group of buildings for the dairy on top of this hill. The farm staff included a superintendent, a resident veterinarian, a farm manager, dairy manager, and a herdsman. Breeding experiments were carried out with the University of Nebraska, and crop experiments—especially in alfalfa—with the University of Delaware. Winterthur's independent water supply included seven artesian wells, a storage tank in the dairy barn with a capacity of 25,000 gallons, a cistern with a capacity of 80,000 gallons, and a pump house.

Fig. 18
Henry Francis
du Pont in 1914
(59.2623),
oil portrait by
Ellen Emmet Rand,
Winterthur Museum.

Although Mr. du Pont added to Winterthur until it reached its greatest extent of 2,400 acres in 1927, he proved to be a thoughtful and considerate neighbor in responding to proposals from the leaders of new community developments as well as from friends and relatives for gifts and sale of his property. Beneficiaries of these gifts and sales included Christ Church, Christiana Hundred (of which Mr. du Pont was Senior Warden from 1928-1946, when he became honorary Senior Warden for life), the Guyencourt Residential Development, the new Wilmington Country Club, the Methodist Country House, and the Winterthur Corporation. Today, Winterthur comprises about 1,100 acres.

Under Bidermann and the Colonel, the Winterthur herd existed primarily to supply dairy products for the estate. When Henry Francis du Pont took over the management of the Winterthur Farms from his father in 1914 (Fig. 18), he announced a more demanding objective—to

Fig. 19 Foundation Animals of the Winterthur Herd, *photograph by Strohmeyer, New York, c. 1922, Winterthur Museum.*

develop a better and perhaps even a perfect breed of Holsteins. When the Colonel replied to this, "It won't cost as much as owning a yacht and it might do a lot for humanity," he was at least half right. Through its sale of purebred bull calves, Winterthur Farms has added finer type, higher production and consequently greater value to herds not only in Delaware, but all over this country and in Canada, Puerto Rico, South America, Australia, and Japan. And in so doing, it has broken a number of world records, establishing itself as not only one of the largest and the most successful of the registered Holstein breeding establishments in America, but one of the finest, for its size, in the world.

Mr. du Pont began with the revolutionary principle of thoroughgoing in-breeding. He had studied the ability of certain breeds of cattle to conform to type in successive generations, reviewed the experience of certain early English breeders who pioneered in the effort to achieve purity of inheritance, and he studied Dr. Helen Dean King's success in inbreeding full brother and sister matings of rats for twenty-five generations with impressive improvement in quality. His bold decision was to secure the best family group of Holsteins possible and to defy accepted doctrine by breeding strictly within that bloodline.

A careful search for the ideal foundation herd was immediately undertaken. After considerable study, a promising possibility was found in the Spring Brook Bess Burke family owned by the Schroeder Farms in Moorhead, Minnesota, whose records established it as among the very finest of the Holstein breed for size, type, and production. In 1916 Mr. du Pont

Fig. 20 The Dairy Barns, 1918-1930, *photograph by J. Victor Dallin, Philadelphia.*

visited the Schroeder Farms and confirmed his opinion, and in 1917 he secured a half interest in one of the Schroeder sires and a son of Spring Brook Bess Burke 2nd, King of the Ormsbys. The following year, he purchased the entire remaining immediate family of five cows—Spring Brook Bess Burke 2nd, her two daughters, a granddaughter, and great-granddaughter, and soon acquired King of the Ormsbys outright (Fig. 19). An intensive program of close line breeding was then adopted. As soon as the inbred bulls were old enough, daughters of King of the Ormsbys were bred back to them almost indiscriminately. The herd expanded rapidly. In 1915, before the foundation family arrived, it numbered 75; by 1920, 300; by 1923, 450 cows. When it comes to deciding which calves to keep for breeding and which to sell, Holstein breeding is an art, and Mr. du Pont studied his herd like an artist.

Meanwhile, Mr. du Pont had undertaken to construct a complete set of model dairy barns (Fig. 20) and these were ready to house his new breeding herd by the time it arrived at Winterthur in 1918. The main barn, which was 319 by 40 feet, houses 152 stanchions plus 12 box stalls; under these were a beet cellar with a capacity of 5,000 bushels, and two tanks supplying water for all the farm buildings; it had a storage capacity of 344 tons of hay, 134 tons of straw, and 240 tons of feed, and at its ends were three large silos. Dampness was prevented under the cows by special dead air chambers, and a complete change of air every six minutes was effected by a forced ventilating system. Other facilities of the dairy, similarly ventilated, included a test barn equipped for 19 head with an attached feed room; a calf barn with a capacity of 135 head where an even temperature was maintained throughout the year; a heifer barn, bull barn, and six barns for wintering young stock; a creamery with a capacity of 10,000 lbs. of milk a day conveyed to its top floor from the barn by an electrified cable tramway, equipped to make butter and certified milk, and complete with a bottling room, an 8-ton ice plant, a cold storage room, and a laboratory for the chemical and bacteriological examination of all milk produced. These facilities permitted the proper stabling of over 400 head of cattle. With access to several hundred acres of excellent pasture land and spring-fed streams, cared for in modern barns by specially trained attendants, within easy reach of three railroad systems and four seaports, the physical conditions for a successful breeding operation were present.[42]

Three special developments in the Holstein dairy world were fully utilized to develop the Winterthur herd: new theories of animal nutrition, the Babcock test for determining butterfat content, and the Advanced Registry (AR) testing promoted by the Holstein-Friesian Association of America which provided an accurate means of comparing productivity in milk production. With a few exceptions, all cows were production tested. The first AR test at Winterthur was completed in December, 1914, the first yearly test in 1918, and the program was continued until 1955. At first all Holsteins on AR test were fed and milked four times daily. In 1932 Winterthur achieved another first among major dairies by going back to the old-fashioned, "dirt farmer" method of two feedings and two milkings a day. The innovation was prompted partly by the destruction of the Main Barn by fire in 1930, partly by depression-forced economy, and partly through a new sales strategy in a more competitive market. Everyone predicted that no records would be made on the two-milkings-a-day (Class C) basis, but they were. In 1933, one of the Winterthur cows ran up a productivity record of Class C that created a sensation in the dairy world. By 1948, the herd had achieved 1,450 AR records in 31 years of continuous testing. Seventeen men were at one time employed exclusively for milking; in 1931, milking machines were installed. The dairy is now producing 5,000 lbs. of milk every two days for shipment, and retaining 300 quarts for use on the estate. For many years, part of this output was bottled as a special milk for infant feeding and for high class table use, and was sold by the Clover Dairy Company as Winterthur Special Holstein Milk. More recently Winterthur milk has been sold to Sealtest, a division of the National Dairy Company.

In two programs of competitive grading in the Holstein-Friesian Association, Winterthur proved itself preeminent. In 1922, the Association instituted an annual Honor List for Breeder, Owner, and Sire, and Winterthur appeared regularly on this list for the next 28 years. In the first year, Winterthur was 31st for Owner and farther down the list for Breeder and Sire. Within four years, however, it was Leading Honor List Owner and Breeder, and on its way to the very top. During the next 22 years, Winterthur was seventeen times the leading Honor List Owner and Breeder. During the 19 years between 1929 and 1947, the Winterthur Herd made "Grand Slams" (first for Breeder, Owner, and Sire) 11 times, twice win-

[42] *Winterthur Farms, Winterthur Delaware* (n.p., privately published, n.d., in two editions, c. 1925, c. 1930); *History of the Holstein Herd at Winterthur Farms* (n.p., privately published, n.d.)

WINTERTHUR TAKES ALL THREE

FOR THE THIRD SUCCESSIVE YEAR

Leading Honor List Sire for 1938
Leading Honor List Owner for 1938
Leading Honor List Breeder for 1938

232
P
O
I
N
T
S
1938

284
P
O
I
N
T
S
1937

Fig. 21
A Grand Slam
for the Herd,
1938, Winterthur Museum.

Winterthur Bess Ormsby Great
Son of KING OF THE ORMSBYS from BESS JOHANNA ORMSBY
Leading Honor List Sire 1937 and 1938 — Second in 1934, 1935 and 1936

ning the three top honors for three years running (Fig. 21); during four additional years of this period, it was awarded two firsts and one second. No other breeder in the country even remotely approached this record, and nothing could better indicate the balanced and coordinated character of Winterthur's breeding program.

A second program of competitive grading was instituted in 1929 as an official classification of herds for type. Using a score card of points, cows and bulls both were scored by appointed officials, and were graded from Poor to Excellent. Bulls whose daughters excelled in both type and production were designated Gold Medal Sire. Winterthur was among the first herds in the country to apply for classification, and, for the 164 head classified, received one of the highest scores ever recorded for a herd of this size. Another record—five bulls in one herd designated Gold Medal at the same time—has never been equaled. Moreover, Winterthur has had three Gold Medal sires each with three Gold Medal sons.

During its fifty years of active competition, the Winterthur herd has won a bewildering number of honors of which a few only can be mentioned. Two of the herd cows (Spring Brook Bess Burke 2nd and Bess Johanna Ormsby) became the leading dam-daughter pair in the breed. In 1933, one of the cows (Winterthur Boast Ormsby Ganne) achieved a world's record for cows milked twice a day. The following year individual cows won both the 3½-year old and the 4½-year old records for the breed. In 1937, Winterthur Holsteins held eight of fourteen possible U. S. Champion records. In 1940, at the National Dairy show, in competition with breeders from all over the country, daughters of King Posch Ormsby of Winterthur won the Get of Sire Class, and, teamed with two daughters of Winterthur Bess Ormsby Great, won first place in Best Dairy Herd and Best Three Females Bred by Exhibitor. The following year, at Memphis, Tennessee, Winterthur again won the Get of Sire Award as well as the Production Get of Sire, and placed in the money in every individual class entered. In 1942, one of the cows (Winterthur Dad Donsegis Inka Jasa) had made the highest score ever made by any cow of the breed. In 1948, one of the bulls (Posch Ormsby Fobes 14th), through the production of his daughters, had made the highest score ever reported by any sire, and became the only five-time winning Honor List Sire in the history of the breed. In 1951, one of the cows (Winterthur Zeus Fobes Cajalo) was in first place for the year for one single lactation with one of the highest scores ever earned by any Holstein.

When Mr. du Pont entered into a very successful experiment in artificial insemination with the University of Nebraska, the latter became interested in studying Winterthur's breeding methods. In 1953 appeared a careful review of this program and its achievement, backed by an exhaustive statistical analysis of production published by the University's Agricultural Experiment Station,[43] and copies of this were distributed to every key agricultural center in the world. It recognized, as of major importance, Mr. du Pont's "foresight in planning and persistence in carrying out the program." In 1962, the Holstein-Friesian Association of America gave to Mr. du Pont its highest award, the Progressive Breeder's Registry Award "in recognition of achievement through an improved breeding program based on production testing, type classification, and herd health for the advancement of Holstein-Friesian cattle." The award was repeated in 1963.

It was a third interest, pursued by Henry Francis du Pont with equal or greater zeal than farming and horticulture, which eventually led to the founding of the Winterthur Museum—an interest in collecting examples of the early American decorative arts. His plan was a simple and sound one —to acquire interiors from old houses and to furnish them with appropriate and authentic furniture and accessories, not for mere display, but to be used and enjoyed as the settings of his own home. The first interiors came from the Eastern Shore of Maryland, and were incorporated into a residence designed for him at Southampton, Long Island, by the architect John W. Cross, which was named Chestertown House. On his inheritance of Winterthur at the end of 1926, the development of the plan was continued here. Mr. du Pont's motivation and purpose were clear. "It seemed to me," he recorded, "that early-American arts and crafts had not been given the recognition they deserved. Serious collectors had for too long focused their attention on Europe and the East, to the exclusion of this country. I hoped, therefore, by preserving under one roof examples of architecture, furniture, and widely divergent early-American materials of all kinds, interest in this

[43] H. F. DAVIS, WILLIAM REED, MOGENS PLUM, "Winterthur: A Study in Breeding Dairy Cattle," Miscellaneous Publication 2, Agricultural Experiment Station, University of Nebraska, November, 1953.

Fig. 22   Winterthur House From the March Bank, After 1930, *Winterthur Museum.*

field would be stimulated and that the magnificent contribution of our past would be helped to come into its own." [44]

The years 1927 to 1931 were ones of the most intense planning and organization. Mr. du Pont's ambitious program called for dramatic new developments at five points simultaneously: a remodeling and extension of his ancestral home to house a vast new assembly of period rooms; the acquisition of this interior architecture from early American houses; the assembling of the objects to furnish these interiors; new landscaping of the area east of the residence; and the creation of a tax-exempt corporation to receive these and other properties if and when it should become desirable to transform the private collections into a public museum.

The remodeling and extension of the old house were begun in the summer of 1929 and completed early in 1931, and were so extensive that Mr. du Pont and his family had to move to the old Bidermann farm house building close by while it was in progress. Five hundred workmen were involved in this complex operation, including one hundred stonecutters and masons, and up to a hundred carpenters. Much of the stone was quarried on the Winterthur grounds. The basic objective was to enlarge the interior area of the house by 200% through the erection of a wing to the south of the old conservatory. Among the many changes this necessitated were the removal of this conservatory and the construction of a new glass-enclosed one where the first porte-cochere on the north façade used to be (Fig. 22);

[44] H. F. DU PONT, Foreword, *American Furniture, Queen Anne and Chippendale* (New York: Macmillan, 1952), p. v.

Fig. 23 Winterthur House From the West, After 1930, With South Wing Added in 1960, *Winterthur Museum.*

and a relocation of the main entrance to the building from the north facade to the middle of the new west facade (Fig. 23) reached by a handsome new driveway. When completed, the new wing extended 150 feet down the hillside to the meadow, rising nine stories high at its southern end.

In addition to this tremendous enlargement of the family residence, the visual effect of its exterior was transformed. In conformity with its new mission—to house a collection of the early American arts—the ornate elegance derived from European Renaissance styles was replaced by a new simplicity based on eighteenth-century American architecture. Two country residences built near Philadelphia—Port Royal in 1762 and Woodlands in 1788—contributed substantially to Winterthur's "new look." From Port Royal came stone cornices, quoins, windowsills, Palladian windows, doorways and facades which were worked into the new east and west walls, and two dormers which were later installed in the roof of the cataloguing, receiving, and model addition, and which were the model, somewhat enlarged, for all the new dormers now replacing the old Francis I-type dormers. From Woodlands came models for key elements in the new Dining Room Porch and the Conservatory. Finally, in conformity with this transformation, the elaborate Spanish roof tiles were replaced by simple terra-cotta ones. Although the new structure—always more than half concealed by the magnificent foliage of surrounding trees—was certainly massive and imposing, nevertheless its plain stucco walls, brightened by the maroon of the shutters and the brick red of the roof, gave a general impression of simple utility.[45]

---

[45] For a more detailed analysis of the changes made in the Winterthur house 1884-1930 see "The Architectural Development of Winterthur House" by Jonathan L. Fairbanks elsewhere in this issue of *Portfolio.*

Fig. 24
Winterthur House,
East Terrace,
Winterthur Museum,
1954.

The second important change to be made was a new landscaping of the area between the new wing and the old rose garden which resulted in an upper terrace supported by massive concrete walls, joined to the old sunken garden area by two handsome flights of stone stairs. The upper terrace was level with what at this point became the fourth floor of the new wing, and was about an acre in size. With its slate walks, its encircling stone balustered railing and gazebo, it formed a superb setting for the six giant poplars and single beech which shaded the entire area (Fig. 24). The terrace could be particularly well enjoyed from the flagstone pavement outside the Vauxhall Room, the east end of the Port Royal Entrance Hall, the Stamper Blackwell Porch, and the great Dining Room Porch on the fifth floor which also commanded a superb view across the Rose Garden to the valley beyond. At the south end of the terrace, a flight of stone stairs descending in several ramps opened, through handsome wrought-iron grilled gates, onto the Rose Garden itself. At the northeast end, a second flight of steps, lined with box, descended past a large sundial through another wrought-iron gate onto the new swimming pool.

Below the terrace, three quite different areas were developed into a subtle unity: the formal rose garden, the large, new swimming pool above it, and the water course laid out in the run. The large, new swimming pool and its two bath houses replaced the smaller pool and garden houses. There were three terraces below the pool, the present one with its grass center and two wide herbaceous borders, the second one now a parking space with only the three wisteria arbors remaining, and the third one now also a part of the parking area with the original wrought-iron grill gates at one end and the wall fountain and pergola at the other serving as reminders of the past. Above the pool, in the woods to the east of the steps and path going to the house, were built two goldfish ponds. The upper and bigger one, fed by one of three springs in this area, was placed just below a steep bank where a nursery recommended by Miss Marian Coffin built a series of small waterfalls among the rocks. Unfortunately, over the years, the pools sprang leaks. A surprising number of plants, started on the bank, have disappeared with the exception of the lovely yellow corydalis, which has seeded itself. One enjoys, however, looking at the ivy and sarcococca, as well as the myriad *Chionodoxa luciliae* planted along the curving path above and around the first pond. The numerous lead putti, tanks, and sundials, and the iron railings and garden furniture placed along the winding footpaths add visual delight as well as convenience to the whole area.

Even before the construction of the new wing was begun, the acquisition of architectural elements from early American homes to be assembled in the new building had begun. From 1927 to 1931, interior woodwork from at least ten houses built between 1730 and 1762 in New Hampshire, Pennsylvania, New Jersey, Maryland, and Virginia was acquired, and this was used to provide the interior architecture for some twenty-three period rooms which were installed during 1929-30, and one during 1931. Among the first houses acquired were Belle Isle from Boer, Virginia; Port Royal near Frankford Junction, Pennsylvania; and Readbourne in Maryland. Some of the houses acquired were in a sadly neglected condition, others were condemned to demolition.

The original height and width of the interior architecture of the rooms from these houses was to be retained in the Winterthur installation, as well as the original location of the doors and windows. In this delicate and exacting undertaking, Mr. du Pont had the services, first, of Albert Ely Ives, a Wilmington architect who also designed the new wing; when Mr. Ives moved to Honolulu in the mid-thirties he was succeeded by Thomas Waterman, a thoroughly experienced American architect and architectural historian who had been associated for six years with Cram and Ferguson in Boston, and who entered fully into the delicate operation involved. As the new floors of the outer shell of the wing were fitted with fine old paneling, handsome mantle pieces, beams, and cornices, the resulting rooms were furnished with objects which Mr. du Pont had been collecting since 1923, and some of which were transferred here from his Southampton home. Since the architecture of several of the first rooms dated from 1750 to 1790, much of the furniture which Mr. du Pont acquired in the first years was of the Chippendale style. In this furnishing, Charles O. Cornelius, associate curator of American Art in the Metropolitan Museum, served as consultant.

The final part of this ambitious plan was the establishment of the Winterthur Corporation, chartered in 1930 as a charitable and educational

Fig. 25   Winterthur House From the South, 1930, *Winterthur Museum.*

foundation. It would be ready to take over the building and the collections if and when these should be made part of a museum—surely not before Mr. du Pont's death, as he then thought. Early in 1931, Mr. du Pont and his family could move back into their transformed home (Fig. 25), and they immediately approved of their new early American surroundings.

New room installations and new additions to the building continued to be made between 1931 and 1951. By 1946, Mr. du Pont had created fifty-six new period rooms and hallways. It was during 1947-48 that he came to realize that his home would probably soon become a museum open to the public.[46] Immediately he undertook a final series of twenty-two room installations, thus utilizing almost all the remaining space available for the purpose. In addition, he provided a visitors' dining room and sitting room on the third floor, and in 1951 built a new visitors' entrance at the south end of the building. Also during 1946-48, he built a small, new wing at the southeast end of the building with carpenter and paint shops on the ground floor and storage facilities for curtains, carpets, and bedspreads above.

In 1949, Mr. du Pont took the important step of beginning a systematic photographing and cataloguing of the collection. To this end he brought to Winterthur two men who were to leave a deep impress on the institution. The first was Joseph Downs, who came directly from the curatorship of the American Wing of the Metropolitan Museum of Art where he had served for nearly twenty years. Before this, he had been curator of decorative arts at the Philadelphia Museum of Art, and earlier had been on the staff of the Museum of Fine Arts in Boston, having graduated from

---

[46] H. F. DU PONT, "The Building of the Winterthur Museum," *loc. cit.,* p. 11.

Fig. 26
Henry Francis du Pont
and his Grandson, 1951,
photograph by Ivan Demetri.
Coll. Henry Francis du Pont.

its museum school in 1921. Mr. Downs had been an active and productive scholar, supervising the installation of important rooms in the American Wing, serving as advisor for key restoration projects in New York City, and writing a series of distinguished exhibition catalogues. When he came to Winterthur, he was generally recognized as the outstanding authority on the American decorative arts.

The second person brought to Winterthur in 1949 to inaugurate its first professional staff was Charles F. Montgomery, a graduate of Harvard and a close friend of Mr. Downs, who had enjoyed an active career as antiques collector, dealer, and professional consultant, and whom Mr. du Pont had known since 1937. Making the pictorial record was placed in the hands of Gilbert Ask, a skilled photographer who had worked with Joseph Downs at the Metropolitan Museum; for leading architectural firms such as Skidmore, Owings, and Merrill, and Harrison and Abromowitz; and magazines such as *House and Garden,* and *Progressive Architecture.* For over a year, the three men lived in the old Bidermann farmhouse below Mr. du Pont's residence.

When, during 1949-50, it was decided to open the Museum to the public a year hence, Mr. du Pont built a new house designed by Thomas Waterman on the spot formerly occupied by the first Bidermann farmhouse, and moved his family into it at the end of 1950 (Fig. 26). On January 18, 1951, the former residence which housed his collections was deeded to the Winterthur Corporation without its contents, and a week later the directors of the Corporation appointed Joseph Downs curator, and Charles F. Montgomery associate curator and executive secretary of the Winterthur Corporation in charge of the operation of the Museum. On October 30, with an impressive ceremony, the Winterthur Museum was opened to the public.

Mr. du Pont's active interest in the American arts, in the restoration of old houses, and in the preservation of our national heritage not only gave the new Museum a rich legacy of associations and loyalties, but brought Mr. du Pont many honors and offices. He became a member of the Board of Governors of the Philadelphia Museum of Art; a member of the Advisory Council of the Museum for the Arts of Decoration of the Cooper Union for the Advancement of Science and Art; a trustee of the Antiquarian and Landmarks Society, Inc., of Connecticut, of the Society for the Preservation of Long Island Antiquities, Inc., and of the Archives of American Art; a member of the National Trust for Historic Preservation, the American Philosophical Society, and of the Walpole Society; chairman of the Furnishings Committee of the John Dickinson Mansion, chairman of the Fine Arts Committee for the White House, and member of the Council of the American Museum in Britain. He has received the George McAneny Historic Preservation Medal of the American Scenic and Historic Preservation Society, the Medal of American Decorative Arts of the 17th and 18th Centuries from the Preservation Society of Newport County, a citation from the Philadelphia Museum College of Art, and the Louise du Pont Crowninshield award of the National Trust for Historic Preservation. Several universities have also bestowed on Mr. du Pont their highest awards in recognition of his services to his countrymen. He has received honorary degrees from Yale University, the University of Pennsylvania, the University of Delaware, and Williams College. Yale's citation included an apt tribute: "You have shown how the judicious and studious collector can instruct the learned and edify the many."

These actively pursued interests in horticulture, stock breeding, and collecting did not prevent Henry Francis du Pont from continuing his family's participation in the management of the Du Pont Company. He became a member of the Bonus and Salary Committee in 1914, was elected a director of the Company in 1915, and served on its Finance Committee from 1916 to 1943. Meanwhile, from 1918 to 1944, he was a director of General Motors Corporation, serving as a member of its Finance Committee from 1918 to 1937.

For one hundred and twenty-five years Winterthur has been a beautiful, productive, pioneering estate. The natural charm of its wooded hills and fertile lands has been enhanced by the careful cultivation of trees, shrubs, flowers, and lawns by its successive owners. In this lovely setting, three quite different avocations have each been brought to a point of excellence. The first, scientific farming, was begun by Antoine Bidermann and further developed by Henry A. and Henry Francis du Pont. The second, gardening and horticulture, was first seriously undertaken under the Colonel, and carried forward by his son. The third, early American decorative art, was the special love of Henry Francis. Under the latter, all three—the Winterthur Farms and the Winterthur Herd, the Winterthur Gardens, and the Winterthur Collections—have earned a world-wide reputation for outstanding and pioneering achievement which has inspired and instructed the practitioners of these three arts everywhere. Meanwhile, the generations who have lived here have evidenced a taste in industrial leadership, in public service, in letters, and in hospitality which exemplifies one of the finest traditions in our American way of life. Winterthur has become a lustrous chapter in the history not only of the du Pont family, but in the history of Delaware and of the United States.

The First Ten Years of
WINTERTHUR
as a Museum

By CHARLES F. MONTGOMERY

On January 1, 1951, the Directors of the Winterthur Corporation became trustees of a building which had long been the home of Henry Francis du Pont; of the unparalleled collections of arts of the American home which he had been gathering for the preceding twenty-eight years; and of certain funds for the operation of a museum.

These facts concerning the beginning of the Henry Francis du Pont Winterthur Museum are well known, but to those intimately connected with the enterprise there was a legacy from Mr. du Pont's own ideals as a collector which became a tradition powerfully influencing the character of the Museum during its first eleven years. These special qualities may be summarized in part as:

1. Standards of excellence supported by superb taste and discrimination; in short, the will to perfection fused with the ideals of the cultured and humane gentlemen that shaped the thinking of the cultivated minds of seventeenth-century England and France, and were the heritage of the leaders of early America.

2. Dedication to collecting and to the belief that this enterprise was important and worth doing, and that in a changing world it must be done now or it would forever be impossible.

3. Zeal and the drive to make progress and to improve—with everlasting work and attention to details.

4. The means, and the daring to commit them to the accomplishment of the vision.

These were the assets of the Winterthur Corporation and of the Museum on January 1, 1951. The task then was for the trustees and staff to

Henry Francis du Pont,
Lammot du Pont Copeland,
and Governor Caleb Boggs
*before the great
carved eagle in
the conservatory
on the occasion of
Patriot Day ceremonies,
April 19, 1955.
(Photo: Harry A. Lemmon)*

create an institution and program that would carry forward the hopes of the founder that this building and these collections would show present-day Americans "how earlier Americans lived." This task was two-fold:

1. To care for and extend the collections.
2. To give the objects in these collections, individually and collectively as period rooms, meaning as representations of the taste and of the way of life of our forbears and of the creativity of the artists and artisans who filled the needs of early Americans.

Upon the opening of the Museum, there was an overwhelming demand on the part of the antiques collector and the general public to see Winterthur. To have satisfied this demand could have been all-engrossing. However, just at that time American civilization programs were blossoming in our universities, and it was felt that Winterthur could contribute to this movement the addition of the study of the arts of the home. In these arts we believed, and still believe, lay the mainstream of aesthetic expression in early America. By embarking upon the Winterthur Program in Early American Culture with the University of Delaware, Winterthur committed itself to a teaching program which was to broaden its horizons from that of the antiques-minded to a historical program with standards of university scholarship. It was to undertake not only "the fostering both at home and abroad of an understanding and appreciation of American arts," but to attempt to provide the scholarly apparatus necessary to a center for the study of American decorative arts and early American culture. This was to involve a continuous extension of knowledge about the objects and the sociocultural context in which they were made and used.

Administration

Although our initial step in education was an important one, a primary task was to find a staff of intelligent and talented men and women and to establish an administrative framework within which they could work effectively and in harmony. Ours was the obligation not only to learn about the collection but also to interpret it as art and as cultural history to the general public through publications and tours and specifically to teach the Winterthur fellows and guides, the latter in turn to interpret the collections to the public.

In establishing any administrative framework human relationships are all-important. In our case many were involved: staff to trustees, staff to founder, staff to each other, staff to guides, guides to the public, Museum to the University, Museum to graduates, Museum to other institutions. To make these relationships sound and effective, it was necessary to establish such means of communication as board reports, the *Winterthur Newsletter* for interchange of information and research, staff meetings, intramural and extramural speeches and lectures, annual seminars for Winterthur graduates, news releases, staff attendance at professional meetings, and answers to a never-ending stream of telephone calls and letters. In all these relationships, I believe the most important single element was enthusiasm in the realization that here at Winterthur was something really wonderful—an unlimited opportunity, opportunity shackled only by our lack of knowledge and imagination. Although it has been written that "to function as an integral unit . . . an institution requires loyalty to the common enterprise and orderly procedures supported by some agreed-upon authority," I am confident that enthusiasm for, pride in, and loyalty to the Winterthur Museum have above all else given impetus to our growth and have sustained us during these pioneering years.

From the beginning, several general administrative objectives were kept in mind and should be noted:

1. To insure use of Winterthur's resources, not only the connoisseur but also the scholar and historian must know of its existence and its wish to serve him.

2. To meet the challenge presented during this period of tremendous growth and change in American museums many steps have been taken to support the movement toward professional standards for museum workers; policies have been formulated to offer time and grants for travel and research, to bring salaries and vacation schedules into a line with those of other scholarly institutions, and to establish pension and hospitalization plans.

3. To assume full responsibility in its professional association, Winterthur staff members were encouraged to attend professional meetings and to participate in a wide variety of organizations; to assist visiting scholars and to play host to professional gatherings which have a kinship with the Winterthur Program. Such encouragement has brought Winterthur into a close relationship with the leaders of such groups as

the American Association of Museums, the Northeast Museums Conference, Association of Art Museum Directors, the College Art Association, Society of Architectural Historians, National Trust for Historic Preservation, American Studies Association, American Historical Association, Fellows in American Studies, the International Institute for Conservation of Historic and Artistic Works, the Society of American Archivists, both national and local library associations, the National Association of Travel Organizations, and the Society of American Travel Writers.

Just as excellence and quality were and are the determining criteria for objects under consideration for the collections, so have they been the goals in everything else undertaken, whether day-to-day operation, exhibition, public lecture, or publication. In public relations, courtesy, dignity, and accuracy have been governing factors. These attributes have brought widespread praise to our guides and all others who meet and deal with the public.

Staff

In the first year, when the staff numbered but five, Joseph Downs's long experience, keen intellect, expertise, and broad knowledge were towers of strength. Nevertheless, it was obvious that, to fulfill the promise of this great collection, manpower and working areas must be added; for, as William Ivins, one of the pioneers of museum scholarship, noted in his address to the Association of Art Museum Directors in Chicago in 1944, great museums are more than buildings, more than collections; they are groups of men—the museum staffs—who use those things as tools for public enlightenment.

Over the years, new personnel came from many sources: The Winterthur Program assured a reservoir of candidates for curatorial and other scholarly activities and a continued source for regeneration; from university staffs we drew a librarian, an editor, a dean of education, and teachers in the Winterthur Program; from public relations activities we acquired an assistant to the director; from business firms we obtained an operations administrator, bookkeepers, accountants, and an engineer. In 1961, the professional staff numbered 23 and the personnel list for the Museum and the Corbit House totaled 126 and 16 respectively, including guides. For each of these people, the transition to work in a museum was a major change; but each of them almost immediately became imbued with the spirit of the institution and has worked with devotion to make this Museum great.

Facilities

Working space for the staff was extended from one small office in 1950 to 36 offices in 1961. First the pantries and servants' quarters, then the ground floor of the new curtain-storage wing provided offices and a staff lunchroom; and, more recently, the South Wing has included not only offices, but libraries, conference room, classroom, photographic studio, guides' sitting room, guests' dining room, and a rotunda for lectures and exhibitions. Space in the Grey Building was found for the cabinetshop; a new carpentershop was built to provide space for the preparation of room installations; and new parking areas were constructed in what were formerly the Rose Garden and the Meadow. The surveys of Edgar J. Meyers, of the Du Pont Company, and Harold Plenderleith, of the British Museum, stressed the need for a new hydrant system and water reservoirs for fire protection. These were completed in 1960. In the same year, the Garden Pavilion was completed, providing much-needed facilities for the ever-increasing number of visitors to the Museum-Garden Tour. The work currently under way to air-condition the entire building is another great forward step toward our goal of providing the best possible conditions and protection for the collections.

To fulfill the promise of the collections, manpower and space were developed; but to realize the potential of the staff, it was important to provide both the climate and opportunity to learn. We needed maximum information about:

1. The best ways to preserve and take care of the collections.

2. The objects, including maker, provenance, style source, meaning, facts about the society in which they were made and used. The latter was especially important to insure accuracy and documentation of our installations and for the interpretation of the objects to the public.

Toward the end of making knowledge available to the staff, three means were utilized:

1. Symposia, seminars, and lectures, for which many experts were invited here to share their knowledge.

2. Staff travel to study, observe, and learn from other collections and people.

3. Development of a library of books, manuscripts, photographs and slides to constitute a reservoir of scholarship, for "no museum can be better than its staff and no staff can be better than its books."[1]

Just as sources of staff lay in a variety of fields and enterprises, so from a variety of related activities came knowledge and experience from which Winterthur has benefited. First and foremost was the university. Not only have we profited enormously from our association with the University of Delaware, but also from personal contacts with the faculty of the University of Pennsylvania and of Harvard, to name but two. Sister museums have helped us on many occasions and in many ways. Staff members of the Museum of Fine Arts, in Boston; the Metropolitan Museum of Art; the Philadelphia Museum of Art; the Victoria and Albert Museum, and many others have come here as lecturers, teachers, and expert consultants. Staff and officials of the Du Pont Company have generously shared their technical knowledge and continue to help us often with specialized advice. Many times each year we have turned to dealers to make gift appraisals.

---

[1] WILLIAM IVINS, JR., "In the Beginning was the Word," *Metropolitan Museum Bulletin* (Summer, 1945), p. 13.

The Collections

The collections and their care and protection have been constantly in mind. During the months when Mr. du Pont's family residence was being converted to a museum, a new numbering and cataloguing system was instituted; a fire-detection system was installed and a close liaison with the local fire company was established; day-and-night guard service was inaugurated; and photography of furniture after oiling and repairing continued as Mr. Downs brought *American Furniture: Queen Anne and Chippendale Periods* to completion. Daily offerings of furniture from dealers and private individuals were reviewed and investigated; an average of several additions to the collections was made each week by purchase. Not only furniture and small objects of all kinds (an estimated 6,000, many of major importance), but also 48 period rooms and exhibition areas have been added, with 6 more interiors on hand for future use.

Whereas in the first years most of the additions were by purchase, the number of gifts has increased annually until, as noted in *Accessions—1960*, 78 donors from 12 states, the District of Columbia, and England could be listed.

As aids to the curator, our exploration of the use of scientific methods and instruments should be mentioned. Winterthur's small projects on wood technology and the use of microphotography for comparison and identification of silver marks have been overwhelmingly useful. The techniques thus developed are now applied to all furniture and silver under consideration for addition to the collections. The exciting new Andelot joint project of the Museum and the University of Delaware to explore further uses of science in museum work offers unlimited possibilities.

Our daily endeavor to bring about a codification of knowledge and to get ideas and the fruits of research out of mind onto paper may seem ephemeral, but will eventually pay dividends just as the codification of policy into a handbook of rules and regulations has enabled many instead of a few to make daily decisions.

Although at the end of my directorship the Museum was officially eleven years old, the enterprise was in fact twenty-eight years older than that; and one of our many efforts during recent years has been to ferret out the facts (concerning objects, rooms, and installations) of those preceding years and to weave them into the history of this new institution.

Conclusion

Those first eleven years may be characterized as a period of trial for all of us—for the directors as trustees and for the staff as management—trial of hundreds of new ways and new approaches to find better methods to make our operation more effective. The directors have given generously of their time, wisdom, and substance to explore and define Winterthur's future. In these first ten years, only a start has been made—much remains to be done to make the libraries and other resources for scholarship worthy of the collections and to give reality to the dream that this Museum become a center for the study of American Arts. This is the task the new administration, under the leadership of Dr. Edgar P. Richardson, has set for itself.

WINTERTHUR CALENDAR

1951-1961

Events in the development and growth of the
Henry Francis du Pont Winterthur Museum
as it evolved from a private collection and family home.

1951

JANUARY

For the establishment of a museum, Henry Francis du Pont gave his ancestral home and surrounding grounds to the Winterthur Corporation — a nonprofit, charitable, and educational foundation established in 1930 under the laws of the State of Delaware.

The officers and directors of the Corporation were:

Beverley R. Robinson, *President*

George W. Jacques, *Vice-president*

Sinclair Hamilton, *Secretary-Treasurer*

Lammot du Pont Copeland	Henry Kirk Greer
Mrs. Lammot du Pont Copeland	Alfred C. Harrison
Mrs. Francis B. Crowninshield	Mrs. Alfred C. Harrison
Edmond du Pont	Walter J. Laird
Henry Belin du Pont	George de Forest Lord, Jr.
George P. Edmonds	Mrs. George de Forest Lord, Jr.
Crawford H. Greenewalt	Mrs. Reginald P. Rose

JANUARY 9

The directors of the Winterthur Corporation made the first staff appointments for the Winterthur Museum: As curator, in charge of the collections, Joseph Downs, who had been for seventeen years curator of the American Wing of the Metropolitan Museum of Art.

Associate curator, Charles F. Montgomery, who had assisted Mr. Downs in cataloguing Mr. du Pont's collection during the previous two years. Mr. Montgomery was also named executive secretary of the Winterthur Corporation, responsible for the operation of the Museum.

JANUARY-
NOVEMBER

Cataloguing and photography were carried forward for *American Furniture: Queen Anne and Chippendale Periods,* press releases, post cards, and special publications in anticipation of the opening of the Museum. This photography was carried out under contract by Gilbert Ask, well-known for his architectural camera studies.

Service areas were soon converted to a dining room for the housekeeping staff (4th floor), offices for staff (7th floor), and Guides' Study Room (7th floor).

A guiding system was developed and seventeen guides were trained by Mr. and Mrs. Montgomery.

A guard system for 24-hour security was established, and a fire-detection system was installed throughout the building.

APRIL-NOVEMBER	In preparation for the opening of the Museum to the public, the following rooms (previously installed with furnishings by Mr. du Pont in another building at Winterthur) were moved to the Museum to areas formerly occupied by bathrooms and living quarters.

Architect's Room   New York Bedroom
Cecil Hall   Visitors' Dining Room
Cecil Sitting Room   Visitors' Entrance
Chapin Hall   Visitors' Sitting Room
Essex Hall   Winterthur Bedroom
Maple-Port Royal Hall   Winterthur Hall
Massachusetts Hall

MAY 15	Alfred C. Harrison was elected vice-president of the Winterthur Corporation; Walter J. Laird, treasurer; and John Marshall Phillips, named a director.
JUNE 11	To assist Mr. Downs in the preparation of the manuscripts for his book on Queen Anne and Chippendale furniture at Winterthur, editorial assistance was necessary. A new post of editorial assistant was created and Miss M. Elinor Betts, formerly a teacher at Goldey Business College, was named to it.
OCTOBER 30	Ceremonies to commemorate the opening of the Museum were held in the Court at eight o'clock in the evening.

Introduction. Mr. Lammot du Pont Copeland, member of the Board of Directors of the Winterthur Corporation.

Invocation. The Reverend William C. Munds, rector, Christ Church, Greenville.

Winterthur Museum as an Educational Institution
Dr. John A. Perkins, president, University of Delaware.

Winterthur and the American Cultural Tradition
Dr. David E. Finley, director, National Gallery of Art; chairman, National Trust for Historic Preservation.

Benediction. The Right Reverend Arthur R. McKinstry, Bishop of the Episcopal Diocese of Delaware.

NOVEMBER 1	The entire issue of the magazine *Antiques* was devoted to the Museum.

Following two weeks of special tours for some four hundred guests, day-long guided tours for the general public began. Five tours of four persons each were conducted daily. Each lasted five to six hours.

1952

JANUARY 8	Lammot du Pont Copeland elected president of the Winterthur Corporation to succeed Beverley R. Robinson who died on September 21, 1951.

William S. Potter named a director of the Winterthur Corporation and elected secretary.

FEBRUARY-MARCH	First lecture series given by Museum staff at Wilmington Y.M.C.A. This cooperative enterprise, with an average attendance of two hundred, was carried on for eight years, terminating only in 1961 with the completion of the Rotunda at the Museum.
MARCH	Publication of *American Furniture: Queen Anne and Chippendale Periods* in the Henry Francis du Pont Winterthur Museum by Joseph Downs. Immediate recognition was given to this first Winterthur book as the major work in its field because of Mr. Downs's great knowledge and the quality and variety of the furniture discussed and illustrated.
APRIL	Trustee committee headed by Mrs. Lammot du Pont Copeland named first group of five fellows to participate in the Winterthur Program to be conducted jointly by the University of Delaware and the Museum. Each received a two-year grant of $4,000 given by friends of the Museum.
MAY 1	With interest in the Museum far beyond expectation, attendance at capacity, and thousands of applications for tickets that could not be filled, clerical and administrative assistance was necessary. A reservation office was established and a bookkeeping and purchasing system inaugurated. To head this important business activity, Wesley A. Adams, with accounting experience and soon to become a Certified Public Accountant, was named office manager.
MAY 6-30	First Museum-Garden Tour. Spring gardens of Mr. and Mrs. Henry Francis du Pont and twenty rooms of the Museum opened to the public without reservations. These tours were started because the regular tours of the Museum were completely booked for 1952 and through half of 1953, and to give the public an opportunity to see the gardens. Guiding was provided by the Junior League of Wilmington with 275 volunteers—a number which grew to 375 in 1960. To provide written material for their instruction, a *Guide* to the rooms shown in the Winterthur Museum-Garden Tour was printed. This was expanded in 1953 and offered for sale to the public. In connection with these tours, arrangements were made with three community churches and the local volunteer fire department to operate a snack bar for their benefit. Although the facilities are far better, the arrangement remains in effect today.
AUGUST 1	A photographic exhibition of Winterthur interiors was shown by the State Department of the United States at the Embassy in London, indicating the interest aroused by the opening of the Museum.
AUGUST 18	The first course of instruction began at the Museum for Winterthur fellows by Mr. and Mrs. Montgomery. Since 1954, several members of the Museum staff have participated in this teaching, with principal responsibility for instruction assigned to the following for the periods indicated:
	Miss Martha Lou Gandy and John A. H. Sweeney, 1954-1956; Miss Gandy and Miss Jessie J. Poesch, 1956-1958; Dr. Albert S. Roe and Dr. Frank H. Sommer, beginning June of 1958.

America Guided by Wisdom. *Drawn by John J. Barrelet, engraved by B. Tanner, Philadelphia. c. 1815. 17⅞ x 24⅛. (58.23.1)*

Allegorical representation of the United States summarizing the hopes and aspirations of a people. In a long "Description" on the print, the symbolic allusions are explained. "Minerva, the goddess of Wisdom, is pointing to a shield, supported by the Genius of America, bearing the Arms of the United States with the motto UNION AND INDEPENDENCE, by which the country enjoys the prosperity signified by the horn of plenty." Also illuminated are the Advantages of Commerce, American Manufactures, Navigation, Industry, and the Progress of Liberal Arts.

Pie Plate. *Pottery, sgrafitto (scratched) decoration. Made by an unidentified Pennsylvania German potter about 1800. Diameter—12. (60.629). (Ex coll. Asher B. Odenwalder.)*

Since much Pennsylvania German decoration is based on medieval Christian symbolism, the Three Fishes glazed in green on a yellow background may have a religious connotation.

Spoon. *Pewter. Length —7 1/6. Joseph France Fund purchase. (61.113)*

Pewter spoons were short-lived and only four or five marked American examples of this seventeenth-century type are known today. The maker's mark, W∴E, is that of William Elsworth, New York City pewterer working 1767-98. Stylistically the spoon is a century earlier because spoon molds continued to be used for a long time.

Hope. *c. 1800. White pine. Height:—52½. (59.64.2, companion to Justice, 59.64.1)*

These carved wooden figures are said to have been used in niches on a Boston custom house. Vigor of carving, flowing robes, and distinctive sandals are hallmarks of the workshop of the brothers Simeon and John Skillen, celebrated for their spirited ship figureheads, and other carving.

Fireback. *Cast-iron. 29 3/16 x 27 1/16. (56.101)*

Cast-iron plates with arched tops were used to increase the efficiency of a fireplace and protect the lining at its back from the flames. This one was cast at an unidentified New England foundry for "Joseph Webb. Boston, 1781."

Baptismal Certificate of Cornelius Dotter. *Chestnut Hill Township, Northampton County, April 23, 1826. 17¼ x 14¼. (61.1105)*

An illuminated pen and ink manuscript of the type known as "Fraktur." Naive in concept, but colorful and strong in execution, the character and use of the flamboyant eagle marks a step in the Americanization of its Pennsylvania German artist.

Chalice with Cover. *Pewter. Over-all height—10½. Gift of Mr. and Mrs. Edgar H. Sittig. (53.97 a, b)*

One of the noblest American pewter vessels. Strong knopped stem, boldness of contour, strength of outline, and the ample bowl and foot are Germanic influences seen in this great covered cup virtually identical to examples bearing the mark of Johann Christopher Heyne, German emigrant, Lancaster, Pennsylvania, 1754-80.

Sugar Bowl. *Pale green glass. Height:—8½. (52.279)*

For sheer style, brilliance of execution, and fitness of material, this imaginative conception has no peer in American glass. Stylistic attributes and history of ownership closely link it to the New Bremen Glassmanufactory of John Frederick Amelung in operation near Frederick, Maryland, from 1785 to 1795.

Silver Bowl. *Made by Jacob Ten Eyck of Albany about 1720 for Evert and Engeltje Wendell. Dimensions: height — 3¾; diameter — 7½; over-all width — 11¼. Gift of Mr. Charles K. Davis. (55.127)*

The generous size, outflaring caryatid handles, and repousse flowers framed within panels are typical of a small group of magnificent late seventeenth and early eighteenth-century silver bowls, fashioned by Albany and New York City silversmiths.

Sugar Box. *Made by Edward Winslow, Boston. Silver. 5½ x 7½. (59.3363 a, b)*

One of the most highly ornamental of a small group of Massachusetts sugar boxes that must be ranked among the masterpieces of American silver. Engraved on bottom, O/DE donum W. P. 1702. Gift of William Partridge to Daniel and Elizabeth (Belcher) Oliver.

Basket. *Philadelphia, 1771-72. China. Dimensions: height—2¾; diameter—8⅛. (59.57)*

One of the most ambitious of the half-dozen known examples of blue-decorated white ware marked with an underglaze "P . . . . " , attributed to the short-lived "China Factory" of Gouse Bonnin and George Anthony Morris. Although not translucent, this piece is porcelain-like in hardness of body and character of glaze.

Bowl. *Porcelain, polychrome decoration. Dimensions: height—6½; diameter—16. (59.149)*

One of the most colorful and fully documented Chinese export porcelain punch bowls made for the American market. Interior inscribed: "Henry Smith, Canton 1794." On exterior in large scale: sailing ship George Washington of Providence on which Smith was supercargo; elements of Rhode Island seal; Great Seal of the United States; and Smith's cypher within a shield.

SEPTEMBER	Daily number of visitors increased to sixty by addition of half-day tours.
SEPTEMBER 16	Dr. John A. Perkins, president of the University of Delaware, named a director of the Winterthur Corporation.
OCTOBER 10	Expansion and cataloguing of the excellent private library of Mr. du Pont became a necessity with its increased use by guides and fellows. Recognizing the importance of the library to the scholarly development of the Museum, the Board of Directors retained Miss E. Louise Lucas, art librarian of Harvard University, as consultant, and established the post of librarian. Miss Helen R. Belknap of the Fogg Art Museum Library was appointed to it.
DECEMBER 15	Opening of the Fraktur and Dunlap rooms to the public. The former, with original painted decoration, from the house built by David Hottenstein near Kutztown, Pennsylvania, in 1783; the latter from the Thomas Chandler house built about 1790 in Bedford, New Hampshire.

1953

JANUARY 5	Staff appointment, instructor in Art History: Mrs. Charles F. Montgomery, a graduate of the Fogg Art Museum course at Harvard University, with museum experience at the Rhode Island School of Design and the American Wing of the Metropolitan Museum of Art, was made responsible for the training and continuing instruction of guides and for the teaching of graduate courses for fellows at the Museum.
APRIL 1	Because of the many activities connected with the opening and operation of the Museum, cataloguing of the collections had come to a standstill. Of the estimated fifty thousand objects at Winterthur, only a small percentage was as yet recorded and described. To assist with this work, Gordon K. Saltar was named to the new post of museum cataloguer. During his first year he began the Museum's first scientific research, the microscopic identification of furniture woods. This was followed by microphotography of silver marks.
	With the many daily visitors the cleaning of the Museum presents problems. Dusting, polishing, and floor maintenance must be carried on regularly in more than a hundred period rooms containing a multitude of fragile objects and delicate antique textiles. Special care and dedication is necessary on the part of every person involved in both the daily maintenance of rooms and the seasonal changes of curtains, slip covers, and carpets. On April 1, George B. Colman, a long-time employee of Mr. du Pont, was named head of the maintenance staff.
	New offices completed for the curator and the editorial assistant in quarters formerly occupied by the housekeeper.
	Two new Museum installations opened to the public—the Wynkoop Room and the Eagle Room.
MAY 1	In connection with the second annual Museum-Garden Tour, special days were scheduled for groups of school children. These tours were first conducted by Junior League Volunteers.

July 1	In 1951 it had seemed that the collections at Winterthur must be nearly complete. What could be found to add new scope to them? Unexpectedly, in response to the new emphasis on American arts brought about by the publicity attendant upon the opening of the Winterthur Museum, interesting objects of special character and quality were offered as gifts or for purchase. Each day brought offers from estates, private owners, dealers, and auction houses. To review and examine them, both at Winterthur and at points all along the Atlantic seaboard, required time and travel. Thousands of objects were considered and some hundreds acquired during the first year and every year thereafter to fill gaps in the existing collections and to furnish new rooms being installed. Curatorial assistance was needed, and on July 1st, Dean A. Fales, Jr., was appointed curatorial assistant.
September 15	Charles K. Davis named a director of the Winterthur Corporation to succeed John Marshall Phillips, whose death occurred on May 7.

During the fall and winter, the first lecture series by fellows and staff for those associated with the Museum was held at the home of Mr. and Mrs. Lammot du Pont Copeland. This series was continued for the next seven years until the completion of the South Wing of the Museum. |

1954

January 22	Twenty-one delegates of the International Congress of Art History and Museology visited Winterthur among other institutions after the close of the Congress in New York City.
January 30	A section of the College Art Association meeting in Philadelphia held its conference in the Court at Winterthur, where four papers on decorative arts were presented.
March 19	The Pewter Club of America met at Winterthur for its twentieth anniversary meeting.
April 20	The first edition of the *Museum-Garden Guide* was published. This forty-page, illustrated guide to the twenty Museum rooms open on the Spring Tour was revised and enlarged by Miss Martha Lou Gandy in 1959 with the assistance of the other members of the staff. Another revision was made in 1961 by Miss Dorothy Greer, and the title changed to *Winterthur in the Spring*. More than 100,000 copies have been printed and sold to date.
April 24	Opening ceremonies of third annual Museum-Garden Tour attended by members and wives of the United States Supreme Court, the Cabinet, and the United States Senate.
May	First Winterthur Seminar on Museum Operation and Connoisseurship for Winterthur Fellows. Over the years, these annual seminars have served to establish and keep alive the bonds of friendship among students and graduates and, at the same time, have provided an opportunity to hear outstanding speakers, exchange information, and discuss common problems.

AUGUST 1   Miss Martha Lou Gandy and John A. H. Sweeney, graduates of the
                Winterthur Program, appointed curatorial assistants.

SEPTEMBER 8   Death of Joseph Downs, first curator of Winterthur Museum.

OCTOBER 1   The directors of the Winterthur Corporation named Charles F.
                Montgomery director of the Museum combining the responsibilities
                of administration and curatorship.

OCTOBER   Extensive hurricane damage to Museum trees.
14-16

OCTOBER 24   To take charge of public relations and advance booking for the
                Museum-Garden Tours, as well as to make arrangements for special
                events, Miss Dorothy W. Greer, with wide experience in publicity
                and public relations, was named assistant to the director.

Conference on the
Place of Objects
and Ideas in Early
American History
*to provide a framework
and approach for
a publication,*
America's Arts
and Skills,
December 6, 1954.

DECEMBER 6   Conference of twenty-two scholars on "The Place of Objects and
                Ideas in Early American History" was held at Winterthur. These
                discussions were to provide a framework and approach for a publi-
                cation, *America's Arts and Skills.*

1955

JANUARY 18   The Joseph Downs manuscript collection established by the Board of
                Directors as a memorial to perpetuate the ideals and scholarship of
                Winterthur's first curator.

MARCH 21	The Winterthur Newsletter started:

MARCH 21   The Winterthur Newsletter started:

1. To give staff and guides basic information about the Winterthur collections as new pieces were installed or as additional information was obtained;

2. To inform members of the Winterthur family of reference and research materials available for their use and to provide a vehicle for disseminating information gained through research by staff, guides, students, or graduates—information that would provide background knowledge for their interpretation of the collections or of the Museum itself;

3. To serve as a permanent record of individual or group activities of a professional nature conducted at Winterthur or connected with the work at Winterthur.

APRIL 18   The first of nine articles on "America's Arts and Skills" appeared in *Life Magazine*. For this series the approach of the Winterthur Program in Early American Culture served as a pattern to show how history can be dramatized through the arts and how art can be better understood through the study of history and related disciplines.

Important Winterthur rooms and objects were illustrated, and seven staff members of the Museum and the University of Delaware were given official recognition for their assistance in this broad-scale attempt to open millions of Americans' eyes "to a national tradition of artistic accomplishment that began in the seventeenth century and continues unbroken today."[1] The series was republished in 1957 in book form by E. P. Dutton and Co., Inc., with an introduction by Charles F. Montgomery.

APRIL 19   Revised edition of the *Museum-Garden Guide* published.

APRIL 19-MAY 29   Fourth annual Museum-Garden Tour opened with Patriot's Day ceremonies. Addresses by Governor J. Caleb Boggs and Lammot du Pont Copeland, with city, county, and state officials—including the Delaware Assembly—in attendance.

MAY 17   Dr. Edgar P. Richardson, then director of the Detroit Institute of Arts, and Dr. Louis B. Wright, director of the Folger Library, named to the Board of Directors.

MAY 23-28   Second annual Winterthur Seminar on Museum Operation and Connoisseurship with lectures and discussions led by John Hayward of the Victoria and Albert Museum and other prominent museum and preservation experts.

JUNE 1   With funds from a special gift of Henry Francis du Pont, a pilot study was begun for a Decorative Arts Reference Library to contain photographs of documented examples of American arts owned by private collectors, museums, and dealers. Such photographs are of great usefulness in the identification of unknown objects and provide basic information for studies of many kinds.

JUNE 6   Charles F. Hummel, a graduate of the Winterthur Program, appointed curatorial assistant.

---

[1] CHARLES F. MONTGOMERY, "Introduction," *America's Arts and Skills* (New York: E. P. Dutton and Co., Inc., 1957) p. 10.

Desk and Book Case. *c. 1790.
Woods: mahogany and white
pine. Dimensions: height—95;
width—37; depth—19½. (56.23)*

*The bombe base with serpen-
tined front which is the highest
expression of the curvilinear
form in American case furniture, the elaborate brass mounts
in the Chinese taste, the rich
sampling of Adamesque ornament and architectural detail,
the superbly carved pedimental
figures of Justice, Commerce,
and Agriculture, all combine to
make this a tour-de-force of
American furniture. Made for
William Barrell, a wealthy Boston merchant.*

Lady's Writing Desk. *c. 1800. Woods:
mahogany, satinwood, and red cedar.
Dimensions: height—62⅛; width—30⅞;
depth—22¼. (57.68)*

*The veneered satinwood door fronts,
mitered at the corners, and inset with
painted and gold-leafed glass ovals (features favored by Baltimore cabinetmakers) and cross-banded satinwood
outlines of drawers and skirt give colorful contrast and distinction to this small
Baltimore desk.*

High Chest of Drawers. *1750-60.
Woods: mahogany and tulipwood.
Dimensions: height—81; width—
39; depth—21¼. (Downs 191).
51.32, (matching Dressing Table,
55.36).*

*The undercut talons, trim over-all
outline, and well-articulated curves
leading the eye to the focal points
of base and pediment suggest the
artistry of design typical of the best
eighteenth-century Newport cabinetmaking.*

Looking Glass. *Philadelphia, 1760-80. Wood: yellow pine. Dimensions: height—55½; width—28.
(Downs 259) (52.261)*

*Original decoration of white paint highlighted with
gold leaf. Joseph Downs described "The fanciful
design of C scrolls, rockwork, and pendants of oak
leaves and flowers" of this masterpiece of American
carving as "the nearest approach in America to the
airy designs of Lock and Copeland, the pioneers in
rococo in mid-eighteenth century England."*

High Chest of Drawers, *inscribed at the
back of the case behind the lower center
drawer: "This was made in y℮ Year 1726
by me Samuel Clement of flushing June 8."
Woods: red gum, ash, elm. Dimensions:
height—72; width—43¼; depth—24½.
(57.512, matching Dressing Table, 57.511)*

*The earliest known piece of New York
furniture documented so well, it provides
evidence of the lingering William and
Mary Style and an insight to its interpretation in New York furniture.*

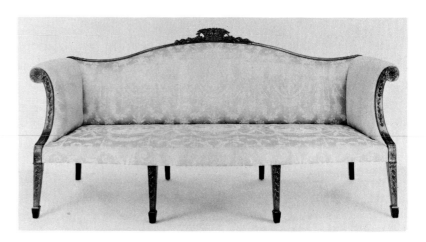

Sofa. *1790-1800. Woods: mahogany, birch, and white pine. Upholstery: pale blue and cream-colored French silk. Dimensions: height—39; width—88; depth—29½. (57.650)*

Delicacy, grace, and beauty characterize this Salem, Massachusetts sofa, enriched with classical ornament carved with the skill and precision associated with the name of Samuel McIntire.

Sofa. *Philadelphia, 1740-50. Woods: walnut, ash, and pine. Upholstery: early eighteenth-century blue silk woven in damask pattern. Dimensions: height—36; length—84; depth—26. (52.264).*

Until this example came to light in 1952, no other American sofa in the Queen Anne style was known. Since that time another, closely related, has been added to the Winterthur collection.

Armchair. *1760-80. Woods: mahogany and American white oak. Dimensions: height—38¾; width —27¼; depth—24¼. (56.30.1) (Ex colls. Cooper Smith Family, Germantown; William West, Hope Lodge.)*

Ample proportions, richly carved ornament, and green silk damask upholstery give this chair an air of opulence, characteristic of the finest Philadelphia Chippendale high-style furniture.

Armchair. *c. 1760-80. Woods: mahogany, American maple, and beech. Upholstery: mid-eighteenth-century brocaded silk. Dimensions: height — 44; width (seat) — 29; depth (seat)—22½. Bequest of Mrs. Francis B. Crowninshield. (58.140.4)*

Sharply raking side claws, block and vase-turned stretchers and knuckled outflaring arms indicate a Massachusetts origin for this rare high-backed predecessor of the more frequently seen "Martha Washington" chairs.

JULY 1   The Index of Early American Cultures, a new approach to the study of American social history (conceived by Dr. Anthony N. B. Garvan and Dr. Frank H. Sommer and based on the principles of the Human Relations Area Files at New Haven) established at Winterthur. Under the directorship of Dr. Garvan, an important study of the Boston culture for the years 1675-1725 was completed during the following three years with major support from the Andelot Foundation and assistance from the University of Pennsylvania and the Smithsonian Institution.

A slide rental program was inaugurated as a further step toward making the Winterthur collections available to others outside the walls of the Museum.

AUGUST 1   Miss Martha Lou Gandy and John A. H. Sweeney advanced to rank of assistant curators.

AUGUST 15   Winterthur was rapidly becoming an educational institution. Not only were staff members teaching graduate courses under university auspices and giving lecture series, but its guides were in a real sense teachers. To coordinate these activities, the post of dean of the Education Program was created. An historian, Dr. E. McClung Fleming, the dean of Park College, was named to the position.

SEPTEMBER 15 Dr. Anthony N. B. Garvan, associate professor of American Civilization of the University of Pennsylvania and author of *Architecture and Town Planning in Colonial Connecticut,* appointed Museum lecturer (on a part-time basis) in the Winterthur Program of Early American Culture.

1956

JANUARY 1   A noncontributory pension plan established for Museum employees by the Board of Directors.

JANUARY 17   The Waldron Phoenix Belknap, Jr., Research Collection of American Painting was established at the Museum with endowment provided by Mrs. Waldron Phoenix Belknap "to the end that Mr. Belknap's research may be available to others and may inspire in them to continue the study of American painting with a view to publication." Mr. Belknap's personal library was included in the gift.

MARCH 1   Eric de Jonge named to new post of building superintendent.

JUNE 4-15   Third annual Winterthur Seminar on Museum Operation and Connoisseurship. The first week was devoted to the broad problems of administration and research and the second to the various techniques—especially those involving the use of scientific instruments—that may be employed as aids to the curator in the preservation and identification of objects. A resumé of the proceedings and of the papers presented by twelve leaders of the business and museum world was published afterwards.

JULY 1   Miss Jessie J. Poesch, a graduate of the Winterthur Program, named curatorial assistant.

AUGUST	The first edition of *Handbook of Rules and Operational Policies* drafted by Dr. Fleming. This was an attempt to codify Museum policies established by the trustees so that decisions could be made on many levels of administrative authority.
OCTOBER 15	Charles Coleman Sellers, distinguished scholar and author of the three-volume study of life and painting of Charles Willson Peale, appointed librarian of the Belknap Library. A. Chapin Rogers, for several years a member of the Print Department of the Metropolitan Museum of Art, began research on Museum records.
NOVEMBER 1	Russell H. Kettell, author of *Early American Rooms* and *Pine Furniture of Early New England,* named consultant on period-room woodwork. Before his death on May 23, 1958, he gave valuable assistance on the removal of woodwork from old houses and its installation in the South Wing, and prepared for the Education Division its first photographic loan exhibit, "A Primer of Artists and Artisans."

1957

JANUARY 15	Wesley A. Adams promoted to new post of operations administrator.
MARCH 1	A museum addition, with enlarged textile and curtain storage facilities and four new offices, completed. Architects: Victorine and Samuel Homsey.
APRIL 23	Ceremonies commemorating Bicentennial of Birth of Lafayette and Opening of "Winterthur in Spring." Addresses given by Lammot du Pont Copeland, president, Winterthur Corporation; The Honorable J. Caleb Boggs, governor of Delaware; The Honorable C. Douglas Dillon, deputy under secretary of state for Economic Affairs; His Excellency, Herve Alphand, ambassador of France to the United States. *Lafayette, The Nation's Guest,* a picture book prepared by John A. H. Sweeney, was published in connection with the special exhibition.
MAY 21	Dean A. Fales, Jr., advanced to secretary of the Museum, and John A. H. Sweeney to associate curator.
JUNE 3-7	Fourth annual Winterthur Seminar on Museum Operation and Connoisseurship. A resumé of the papers presented by fifteen museum specialists was published.
AUGUST 10	"Handbook for Winterthur Fellows" prepared by Dr. Fleming and circulated.
AUGUST 13	Excavation begun for the South Wing of the Museum. This addition (completed in stages during 1959) includes staff offices, a photographic studio, libraries, a rotunda for lectures, sixteen period rooms and exhibition areas for school children and for visitors without reservations. Architects: Victorine and Samuel Homsey.
SEPTEMBER 1	Milo M. Naeve, a graduate of the Winterthur Program, named curatorial assistant upon his return from service in the Armed Forces of the United States.
OCTOBER 1	S. Damie Stillman, a graduate of the Winterthur Program, named assistant librarian of the Belknap Library.

Andirons. *1750-75. American, bell metal and wrought iron. Height—28⅛. (54.92.1,2, with matching shovel and tongs, 54.92.3,4)*

Few designs in American arts are so distinctive, beautiful, or peculiarly American as those to be found in brass or bell metal andirons of the eighteenth and early nineteenth century.

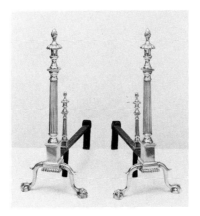

Chest of Drawers. *Newport, Rhode Island, 1765-90. Woods: mahogany and white pine. Dimensions: height—32; width—35¾; depth—20¼. Gift of Mr. and Mrs. William K. Wallbridge. (58.18.1)*

Block-front furniture with a large shell as the crest for each vertical panel has long been considered the greatest American contribution to cabinetmaking. Members of the Goddard and Townsend families of Newport, believed to have originated this design, surpassed all others in the making of splendid chests, desks, and dressing tables with such three-dimensional façades.

Dressing Table. *Massachusetts, 1735-60. Woods: walnut and white pine. Dimensions: height—31⅛; width—33⅝; depth—21¾. (61.142)*

The rhythm of the convex and concave contours of the "Round Blocked" façade is repeated in the top and skirting to give movement and unity to a rare form.

Kas or Cupboard, *one of the few examples of seventeenth-century American inlaid furniture to survive. Owned originally by the Hewlett family of Merrick, Long Island. Woods: red and white oak, chestnut, and white pine. Dimensions: height—70¾; width —57¼; depth—27¼. (52.49)*

Its monumental scale, architectural quality, and boldly patterned panels are reminiscent of Dutch design.

Table with Folding Top, *thought to be of Pennsylvania origin because of a history of ownership in Delaware County, Pennsylvania, and the use of walnut and white oak. Late seventeenth century. Dimensions: height—31; width— 60¼; depth (closed)—23⅝. (54.94)*

The boldness and large scale of individual members, especially of the turnings, place this table as one of the earliest Pennsylvania examples.

1958

JANUARY 21   Alfred E. Bissell named a director and elected treasurer of the Winterthur Corporation to succeed Walter J. Laird who gave valuable service to the Museum until the time of his death on June 3, 1957.
At this time, a broad program was approved by the Board of Directors to strengthen fire-fighting potential. During the next three years, a fire brigade was trained; reservoirs built to store large quantities of water; a hydrant system, auxiliary power plant, and pumping facilities installed; and a fire truck with high rise (eighty-five feet) hydraulic platform purchased.

MARCH 27-29   Fifth annual Winterthur Seminar on Museum Operation and Connoisseurship. Lectures and discussions by Peter Floud, and others, on printed textiles. At this time, Mr. Floud of the Victoria and Albert Museum spent a month at Winterthur studying and identifying the Museum's large holdings of English printed fabrics.

APRIL 28-29   Annual meeting of the Association of American Art Museum Directors held at Winterthur. Attended by sixty members.

MAY 1   *American Silver in the Henry Francis du Pont Winterthur Museum* by Martha Gandy Fales—a catalogue with 143 illustrations of the Museum collection—was published.

MAY 20   Two art historians, Dr. Frank H. Sommer, former coordinator of the Winterthur Program in Early American Culture at the University of Delaware, and Dr. Albert S. Roe, author of *Blake's Illustrations to the Divine Comedy,* were named to the Museum staff as research associates, with curatorial and teaching responsibilities.

JUNE 9   Lorraine Waxman Pearce, a graduate of the Winterthur Program, appointed cataloguer, a position which she held until October 1, 1960.

JULY 1   Dr. Harold T. Plenderleith, head of the Research Laboratory at the British Museum, was in residence at Winterthur for four weeks as consultant on methods of preservation and conservation. Specifically, Dr. Plenderleith was asked to review Winterthur's procedures and make recommendations. As a result of his report, the Board of Directors decided to air-condition the Museum building.

JULY 17-18   Museum Science Seminar. Under Dr. Plenderleith's chairmanship, leading museum scientists in the United States met at Winterthur to discuss areas of scientific research, current practices, activities, and methods being utilized in museum laboratories.

SEPTEMBER 1   Charles F. Hummel, after two years in the Armed Forces, returned to the staff as curatorial assistant with additional responsibility as assistant director of the Index of Early American Cultures.

NOVEMBER 1   Completion of the Kershner rooms installation consisting of the two ground-floor rooms (kitchen and hall) with exterior stone facade from a Pennsylvania German farmhouse built about 1755 and a part of the adjacent 1840 bakehouse with oven. The great Hall is distinguished by its unique boldly patterned plaster-work ceiling.

NOVEMBER 6-8   "New Horizons for Museums" was the theme of the Northeast Museums Conference which met in Delaware, with headquarters at Winterthur for the 148 delegates.

Kershner Parlor, *one of two rooms installed in 1958 from a house built about 1755 near Wernersville, Pennsylvania, and long occupied by Conrad Kershner. Boldly patterned plasterwork ceiling and eighteenth-century Pennsylvania German furniture.*

1959

JANUARY 3	Announcement of H. Rodney Sharp's gift of the William Corbit House with endowment to the Winterthur Corporation. This fine eighteenth-century house, restored and furnished by Mr. Sharp, provided the Museum staff with an unusual opportunity to explore and develop the use of an historic house as an educational instrument.
JANUARY 21	Milo M. Naeve advanced to assistant curator.
FEBRUARY 18	First lecture series in the new South Wing—"The History of Furniture from Earliest Times Through the Nineteenth Century"—given by Dr. Robert C. Smith, professor of Art History at the University of Pennsylvania.
MAY 19	A. Chapin Rogers appointed librarian of the Belknap Library following resignation of Charles Coleman Sellers.
MAY 27	New appointments: Dr. Robert C. Smith, professor of Art History, University of Pennsylvania, named research associate, an honorary title to indicate the affiliation with the Museum of a scholar not on the staff. Mrs. Dean A. Fales, Jr., keeper of silver; and Mrs. Charles F. Montgomery, keeper of textiles. The work of a keeper is curatorial in nature but involves no administrative responsibility.
MAY 28-30	Sixth annual Winterthur Seminar on Museum Operation and Connoisseurship. Following lectures on "Training for Curatorship in Britain," by Dr. W. E. Swinton, president, British Museums Association, and "The History of Art History as a Discipline, with Some

Thoughts on the Study of American Arts," by Rudolph Wittkower, professor of History of Art, Columbia University, there were panel discussions on "Object Analysis and Interpretation" and "Area Interpretation: Arts in the Delaware Valley." A 120-page resumé of the proceedings was published.

JUNE 1   Publication of *Grandeur on the Appoquinimink* by John A. H. Sweeney. This comprehensive study of the William Corbit House, a model for the interpretation of an historic house, is the first book in the Winterthur Series by the University of Delaware Press.

SEPTEMBER 1   Horace L. Hotchkiss, Jr., of the Corcoran Art Gallery, appointed curator of the Corbit-Sharp House which was officially opened to the public on October 12, Odessa Day.

OCTOBER 15   Milo M. Naeve named registrar and secretary to succeed Dean A. Fales, Jr., who resigned to become director of the Essex Institute, Salem, Massachusetts.
To bring the maintenance of the building and the daily care of its contents under one head, George B. Colman was appointed building superintendent.

NOVEMBER 1   A twenty-minute motion picture in color about Winterthur made by the United States Information Service. Translated into forty languages, it has since been shown in American embassies all over the world.

1960

APRIL 1   Publication of *American Colonial Painting: Materials for a History*. Edited by Charles Coleman Sellers from the notes of Waldron Phoenix Belknap, Jr., brilliant amateur American art historian who was the first to grasp the relationship of eighteenth-century American painting and English mezzotints.

APRIL 7-9   Seventeen graduates of the Winterthur Program were the speakers at the seventh annual Winterthur Seminar on Museum Operation and Connoisseurship.

APRIL 26   Revised edition of the *Museum-Garden Guide* was published to mark the opening of the ninth annual Museum-Garden Tour. On this occasion, the newly installed rooms in the South Wing were opened. These include:
Banister Stair Hall from the Banister-MacKaye house, built in 1756 near Newport, Rhode Island, by John Banister.
Carroll Stair Hall with extraordinary painted murals signed "William Price 1831," from an early-nineteenth-century house that served as a tavern for many years in the village of East Springfield, New York.
Charleston Ball Room from the Mansion House in Charleston built about 1772.
Chippendale Bedroom, another room from the Banister-MacKaye house.
Dominy Clock Shop and *Dominy Woodworking Shop.* Both, with original tools, are replicas of the shops used by three generations of the East Hampton, Long Island family of cabinetmakers, working between 1757 and 1845.
Federal Parlor from the Phelps-Hatheway house at Suffield, Connecticut, remodeled and enlarged in 1794-1796 by Oliver Phelps.
Somerset Room from a wing added in the 1790's to the Jerathmael Bowers house of Somerset, Massachusetts.

Dominy Woodworking Shop, *eighteenth and early nineteenth-century woodworking tools and cabinetmaking patterns for determining shapes of furniture legs, chairbacks, etc., used by Nathaniel Dominy IV (1735-1812), his son, and grandson in East Hampton, Long Island. Tools (and the clockmaking tools shown in adjacent Dominy Clock Shop) purchased with funds given by Mr. Henry Belin du Pont.*

Federal Parlor, *from the Phelps-Hatheway House, Suffield, Connecticut. A noteworthy interior with neoclassical woodwork and original French wallpaper from a wing added (1794-96) to an older house by Oliver Phelps.*

Doorway and Porch from Oak Hill at Danvers, Massachusetts, built in 1801 for Captain Nathaniel West and his wife, Elizabeth Derby.
Empire Hall with woodwork from the original section of Winterthur, built in 1839 by James Antoine Bidermann.
New England Kitchen based on the kitchen of a house built at Oxford, Massachusetts, about 1740.
Queen Anne Bedroom from a small house built in Coombs' Alley, Philadelphia, about 1760.
Seventeenth Century Room, the hall, or main room, from the two-room house built near Essex, Massachusetts, about 1684 by Seth Story.
Bowers Parlor from the Jerathmael Bowers house built in the 1760's in Somerset, Massachusetts.
William and Mary Parlor, about 1725, from the Thomas Goble house at Lincoln, Massachusetts.

MAY 17   John A. H. Sweeney advanced to curator of the collections—the first to be appointed since the death of Joseph Downs—and Charles F. Hummel to associate curator. Mrs. Gail Belden and Miss Ruth Y. Cox, a graduate of the Winterthur Program, named curatorial assistants.

SEPTEMBER 28-
OCTOBER 28   "Philadelphia Reviewed," a special exhibition of fifty prints pertaining to Philadelphia, arranged by the 1961 class of Winterthur Fellows. A multilithed catalogue was published.

OCTOBER 8-
NOVEMBER 1   Delaware Library Association held Fall Meeting at Museum.
To develop the manuscript, microfilm, and photocopy holdings of the Joseph Downs Memorial Library, a full-time librarian, Mrs. Elizabeth A. Ingerman, formerly of the Library Company in Philadelphia, was appointed.

DECEMBER 1   The Museum's collection of carved wooden figures was installed on the porch off the Stamper-Blackwell Room and the area renamed the Hall of Statues.

DECEMBER 21-
FEBRUARY
18, 1961   "Accessions 1960"—in the Rotunda and Long Gallery—a special exhibition of 150 objects acquired during the year for the Museum, the Belknap Library, and the Corbit-Sharp House. An illustrated catalogue, *Accessions 1960,* was published.

1961

JANUARY 9   John J. Evans, Jr., named research associate in charge of the Decorative Arts Reference Library. Although working only on a part-time basis, Mr. Evans has greatly increased the holdings, and applied modern methods of information retrieval to the documented photographs in this collection. At the present time, every effort is being made to acquire photographs of American furniture and silver by known makers.
At the conclusion of a year-long study to determine the feasibility of air-conditioning the main building of the Museum, approval was given by the Board of Directors to begin work on this important project, which may require five years for completion.

FEBRUARY 1   The Henry Algernon du Pont Memorial Library reopened after being refurnished to include memorabilia of Colonel du Pont and items pertaining to the history of Winterthur.

Accessions 1960, *an exhibition (December 21, 1960 to February 18, 1961) of 150 objects acquired through gift and purchase for the Museum, the Belknap Library, and the Corbit-Sharp House.*

The Garden Pavilion, *completed in the spring of 1961. Architects: Victorine and Samuel Homsey, Wilmington.*

APRIL 25-   Tenth annual Museum-Garden Tour marked by opening of the new
MAY 27   Garden Pavilion. This building, distinguished by its broad gabled
                roofline and sidewalls of glass, serves as a reception area and has
                luncheon facilities to accommodate three hundred people. Architects:
                Victorine and Samuel Homsey.

Mrs. John F. Kennedy,
*wife of the late
President of the United States,
in the Du Pont Dining Room
before the portrait of
George Washington painted
by Gilbert Stuart in 1796.
Mrs. Kennedy visited Winterthur
as the guest of Mr. Henry F. du Pont,
chairman of the Fine Arts Committee
for the White House. (Photo:
Robert Hunt Whitten Associates)*

MAY 8   Mrs. John F. Kennedy, wife of the President of the United States, visited Winterthur to study its collections and rooms in connection with the refurnishing of the White House.

MAY 11-13   The general theme of the eighth annual Winterthur Seminar on Museum Operation and Connoisseurship was "Expertise for the Curator with Emphasis on Metals and Furniture." Much of the Seminar was conducted by John F. Hayward, deputy keeper of woodwork at the Victoria and Albert Museum.

SEPTEMBER 10   Work on the new Vickers Alcove installation as well as the revision in the Upper Salem Stair Hall completed.
Miss Mary Elizabeth Norton named assistant keeper in charge of the Museum's collection of lantern slides used by the staff and guides for classes and public lectures.

SEPTEMBER 13   Dr. Edgar P. Richardson named director of the Museum following the resignation of Charles F. Montgomery. For the previous sixteen years, Dr. Richardson was director of the Detroit Institute of Arts. Mr. Montgomery named senior research fellow to teach in the Winterthur Program and to devote his time to the study and publication of the collections.

NOVEMBER 15   As aid to Dr. Richardson and in charge of administration, Paul S. Harris, director since 1946 of The J. B. Speed Art Museum, Louisville, Kentucky, was named deputy director.
To develop a program of visual aids and publications of broad scope based on the collections of American arts at Winterthur and elsewhere, John D. Morse, formerly in charge of communications at the Detroit Institute of Arts was named head of a new National Extension Program.

The Architectural Development of WINTERTHUR HOUSE

By JONATHAN L. FAIRBANKS

Few American buildings have undergone as many architectural alterations as has the house from which the Winterthur Museum has grown. This is due in large measure to the varying needs and tastes of its former owners, the changes in popular architectural styles, and, in recent years, to the building's transformation from a private home to a public museum. Even today, the interior woodwork in several of the period rooms is being completely redone; but, with typical modesty, Henry Francis du Pont, the last private owner of the Winterthur house, says in *Winterthur Illustrated* that "some rooms in the Museum are being changed around now."[1] The remodeling in most instances fills out space that had formerly been used as service areas of the Winterthur house, thereby extending the period rooms as far as possible without changing the basic structure of the building. One of the largest current installations is the Billiard Room on the seventh floor, with woodwork of the Federal period removed from an early house recently razed in Baltimore, Maryland. On the same floor an installation is scheduled to include boldly molded paneling from the Gidley house in Newport, Rhode Island, paneling that will provide a handsome setting for eighteenth-century Newport furniture. A Delaware room now being installed on the sixth floor, below the Billiard Room, has woodwork rescued from the demolished Shipley house of Wilmington. This installation preserves woodwork from the family home of wealthy Quaker miller-merchants who played an important part in developing early industry on

---

[1] JOHN A. H. SWEENEY, *Winterthur Illustrated* (Winterthur, Del.: The Henry Francis du Pont Winterthur Museum, 1963), p. 17.

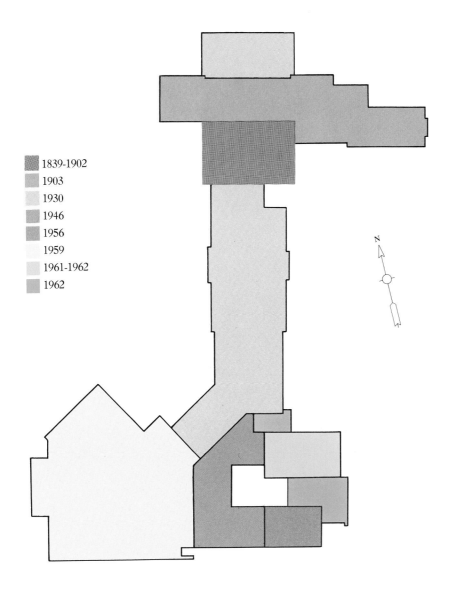

1839-1902
1903
1930
1946
1956
1959
1961-1962
1962

Fig. 1 Plan of the Winterthur Museum, *1839-1963*.

the Brandywine Creek. In effective contrast to the Quaker simplicity of the Shipley Room is a nearby installation with richly colored marbleized woodwork from the William Williams house at Lebanon, Connecticut. On the fourth floor an eighteenth-century window from the Ten Broeck house, from Ulster County, New York, will be installed in an alcove off the Pennsylvania Folk Art Room. Another space scheduled for remodeling is the nearby Dunlap Room, which is to be enlarged to its original dimensions as it existed in a house at Bedford, New Hampshire. The installations going forward and contemplated at the present time suggest the complexity and detailed patterns of growth that have taken place within Winterthur from year to year. The additive character of architectural changes is only a part

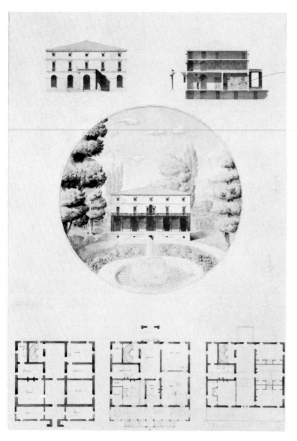 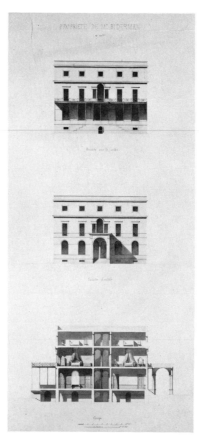 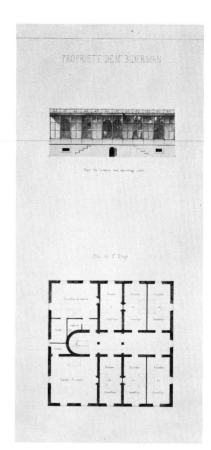

Figs. 2, 3, 4   Drawings, *possibly by N. Vergnaud, c. 1839.*

of the story, however, for builders have removed and rebuilt walls, partitions, or entire façades of the house whenever it was thought necessary. Almost like a living organism, the building has grown and changed with additions and improvements ever since its inception in the early nineteenth century.

The original house at Winterthur was built between 1839 and 1842 for James Antoine Bidermann and his wife, the former Evelina Gabrielle du Pont. Over the years this house was remodeled several times; and today it is completely absorbed in what is now the central, northern section of the Winterthur Museum, roughly in the area of the Chinese and Empire Parlors (Fig. 1, 1839-1902).

A letter to Bidermann from Alfred Victor du Pont, his brother-in-law, indicates that as early as May 23, 1838, Alfred Victor had purchased materials for the construction of a house for the Bidermanns.[2] At that time, however, it appears that no architectural plans had yet been drawn; but Bidermann, who was then in Paris, wrote his brother-in-law that he intended to have an architect there, N. Vergnaud, design his new home. A later letter indicates that work was to have been started in the summer of 1839, but even by January of that year plans had not been received.[3]

Nothing of Vergnaud's work is known; but it is possible that the three unsigned drawings now displayed in the Memorial Library at the Museum

[2] Copy of Letter from Alfred Victor du Pont to J. A. Bidermann, May 23, 1838. Longwood MSS, Eleutherian Mills Historical Library. (Hereafter EMHL.)
[3] Copy of Letter from J. A. Bidermann to Alfred Victor du Pont, January 6, 1839. Longwood MSS, EMHL.

served as the source of the design for the house to be called Winterthur (Figs. 2, 3, 4). As yet, however, no way has been found to relate the designs to Vergnaud. The drawings are in pencil and are tinted with water color; two of them bear the inscription PROPRIETE DE Mr BIDER-MAN [*sic*]. They present a plan not unlike that of the first Winterthur house, but show a building of three stories with five windows across the facade—a larger structure than was built by Bidermann.[4] It is possible Bidermann asked his builder to simplify and scale down Vergnaud's designs with the result that the lateral windows and the central Palladian window were not included in the building.

A bill dated 1842 from William Edwards to Bidermann for painting and glazing his country residence near Wilmington gives evidence that the building was probably nearing completion by that date.[5] This detailed list of materials shows the large number of glass panes used in finishing the residence.

Mr A. Bidermann

	To William Edwards	Vz
1842		
March 9th To Painting Country residence near Wilmington Delaware as per Measure, Bill		$ 971.76
To Glass & Glazing same property. Viz.		
225 lights 20/23 french Cylender 1.00		225.00
15 " 32 inches long—do 1.00		15.00
6—in Small sky light 35		2.10
—Circular sash under. do.		2.50
6 " inside water closet—11/11—20		1.20
—Fancy Sash outside do—		4.00
—do do front door—		2.50
32—in Book Cases 10/15—25		8.00
256—in Green house 11/16—36		92.16
96—in Basement 10/14—23		22.08
21—in Sash doors 10/14—23		4.83
12—in Cellar windows 10/12—18		2.16
8—in Privy—8/10—10		.80
		$1354.09
	measuring—	31.40
		$1385.49
Received up to March 19th—$831.40		
F. g. Smith's bill 97.07 Additional bill		+47.17
		$1432.66[6]

Balance $\dfrac{504.19 + 2.82 = 507.01}{\$1432.66}$

---

[4] The drawings show a building which, in the first-floor plan, measured 64 feet by 64 feet (Fig. 2). A blueprint of Winterthur made in 1901, prior to extensive alterations of the house, shows the exterior dimension of the first floor as 53 feet (front) by 38 feet (side). See Fig. 6. Also, the porte-cochere of Winterthur does not correspond to the porte-cochere shown in one of the drawings (compare Figs. 3 and 5).

[5] William Edwards is listed as a painter in Wilmington at King and Third, with his residence on King, between Fifth and Seventh Streets. Lewis Wilson, *The Wilmington Directory for the Year 1845* (Wilmington, Del., 1845), p. 18.

[6] Bill, receipted April 18, 1842, from William Edwards to A. [Antoine] Bidermann. The E. I. du Pont de Nemours and Company Collection, EMHL.

Fig. 5 North Facade of the Winterthur House, *photograph dated 1883.*

A photograph of the north facade of the house at Winterthur taken about 1883 reveals its probable original appearance (Fig. 5). It was rectangular in shape with symmetrical facades and a Doric porte-cochere on the north side. The Bidermann home was built of brick and stucco in three stories with an attic, or half story, at the third level. The ground floor of the north facade had one window flanking each side of the porte-cochere. Above the second floor, a horizontal stringcourse separated the three windows of the second story from the frieze-like square windows of the third story. This treatment was typical of the period, and was in keeping with the Greek Revival style.

The south elevation of the building had an exposed basement story which was not visible on the north side. This was due to the slope of the ground on which Bidermann constructed his home—a slope that required stairs to reach the garden from the south porch. It was probably the elevated appearance of the south aspect which, in 1858, prompted a writer for the *Delaware Republican* in describing Mr. Bidermann's home to comment that "on the summit of the hill . . . stands the splendid mansion of the proprietor, it is also enclosed with huge oaks and other trees, overlooking the valley and other points, which render it a perfect palace."[7]

It is not known what adaptations and changes were made to the Winterthur house during the years of its first occupancy. When James A. Bidermann died in 1865, the property and home passed to his son James I. Bidermann, who sold it in 1867 to his uncle, Henry du Pont. It was not until seven years later that the first recorded architectural changes were made. A letter dated December 13, 1874, from the Philadelphia architect Theophilus Chandler[8] to Colonel Henry Algernon du Pont tells of some changes that the Colonel's father asked to have made while his son was in Europe on his wedding trip:

> *Ridley Park. Sunday. Dec. 13th—1874*
> *My Dear Colonel—du Pont—*
> *At last we have decided upon the new arrangement of the Winterthur house. I was sorry that you did not see the drawings that were prepared—before you sailed for Europe—Since then a number of changes have been made—and for the best—The new library— and chambers above are to be of the same size as the present conservatory—being built upon its foundations—New foundations are to be built—and the conservatory rolled upon them. In this way the conservatory is kept exactly as it is—the old steps to the garden—removed and a grander staircase made decending [sic] direct upon the lawn—All the other plans for the conservatory were abandoned after great discussion for this. It has the advantage of retaining its old size—does not spoil the windows of either dining room or library—and will still have the effect of the old house—I hope you will not be disappointed*

---

[7] *Delaware Republican,* January 7, 1858 [p. 3].

[8] The following information on Chandler is given by HENRY F. WITHEY and ELSIE RATHBURN WITHEY, *Biographical Dictionary of American Architects (Deceased)* (Los Angeles: New Age Publishing Co., 1956), pp. 117, 118.

CHANDLER, THEOPHILUS P. (1845-1928) Philadelphia, Pa. (F.A.I.A.)

A native of Boston, educated at Harvard, the youth studied architecture in this country and in Paris at the Atlier Vaudremer, and upon his return to Boston opened an office in the city. Later, in 1870, Mr. Chandler moved to Philadelphia and practiced professionally there until late in life when he retired to his home at Ithan (Delaware County), Pa.

During his active years Mr. Chandler planned some commercial buildings and a number of residences, but was better known in the field of church design. His most important ecclesiastical buildings in Philadelphia were the Swedenborgian Church at Chestnut and 22nd Streets and the Bethlehem Presbyterian Church on Broad Street (*). Elsewhere the First Presbyterian Church at Pittsburgh (**) and St. Thomas' Church in Washington, D. C., were built from his plans. Among his various other works were the John Wanamaker residence in Philadelphia at 20th and Walnut Streets, and the Liverpool, London & Globe Insurance Building in that city.

An early member and Fellow of the American Institute of Architects, Mr. Chandler was one of the founders of the Philadelphia Chapter, also helped organize the School of Architecture at the University of Pennsylvania, and served as its first Director.

—*References:* Obit., A.I.A. Journal, Sept., 1928; Information from the Philadelphia Chapter, 1939; Guide to Pennsylvania, Federal Writers' Project (*); Item in the American Architect & Building News, 11/3/1894 (**).

with this adjustment. Your Father is very much pleased with it —and is decided that it is the only way—I will make a little sketch below—and you will see at once—Do not laugh at the grand display of walks and terrace— that I have just scribbled— I am afraid you will have to finish all that—And now while I mention terrace—you will see so many pretty examples of just such arrangement of terrace and lawn—in France—and better still in Italy—Why not make a memorandum?—and find photographs of such as you see—in a similar situation—It would be very pretty and quite grand with the great trees on both sides— I can mention a number of good reasons for the conservatory in the place decided upon—It does not darken the kitchen windows —It is larger than it could be in any other place—In the Summer the glass can be taken out—and it can be used as a grand piazza —Early in the Fall the glass returned—and it will make a most delightful room—opening from the library—All the flower stands are now made and in perfect order—had we made a new conservatory all would have to be changed—This plan will cost at least one thousand dollars less than the one with the piazza in front—conservatory one side—as in the little sketch I made for you the first day we were there—and gives a fine room under conservatory for a laundry—Between the library and conservatory there will be a very large glass door—Thus making the library appear much larger—In the chamber above the library the window will open down to the conservatory roof—just as it does now—the iron railings retained—I will not leave the first floor yet. The hall to be changed as you want it with a large arch —the fire place moved into the centre—a new mantle of walnut— About the hardwood floors—I think you had better wait until you are settled in the house—it is something you can do any time— Your Father would not think of it now—And if made—you would perhaps be disappointed in them—Dumb waiter made— and other small changes on first floor—Second floor—the bath room—it has not been decided yet about its supply of water— other slight changes on this floor—Third floor—stairs to the roof principal change—And now the exterior—after a number of sketches—and examination of the house from the different points of view—and in particular from the meadow and lawn—I have decided not to carry the new portion above the main cornice —But to emphasize the tower with a bold balustrade above the cornice—breaking the sky line and forming a railing around the roof. If the tower had been one story higher—it would have appeared too narrow for its width and height—that is it would not have projected enough from the main building—I can soon send you drawings of interior and exterior—I know how anxious you are about it all—I can soon give you a more detailed account of every little thing—Say to your Wife—that on Thursday—I went through the house with Willie—let the sun in the Windows —found two nests of flying squirrel—and thought we had never seen a brighter prettier place—

> *Sophie sends her love*
> *Sincerely yours, T. P. Chandler*[9]

[9] Letter from T. P. Chandler to H. A. du Pont, December 13, 1874. The Henry Francis du Pont Winterthur MSS Collection, EMHL.

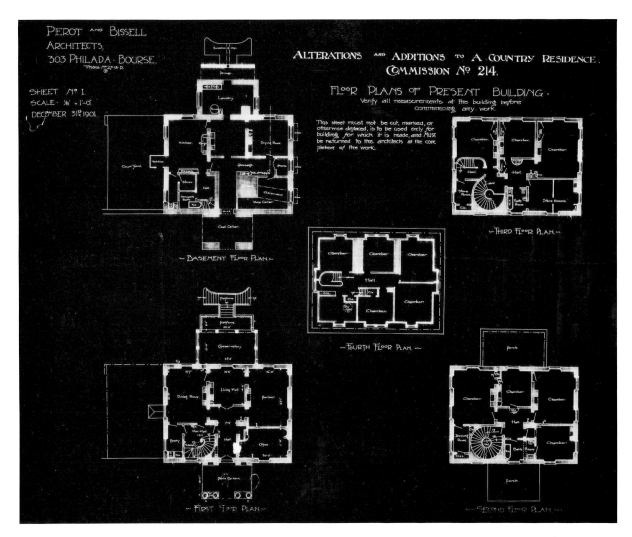

Fig. 6 Plans of the Winterthur House, *blueprint by Perot and Bissell, dated 1901.*

It is evident from this letter that most of the changes recommended by Chandler at this time were internal improvements. A plan at the end of the letter shows a new library between the conservatory on the south and the main body of the house; but apparently this design was not carried out, for such an arrangement does not appear in a later plan of the house made in 1901 by the architectural firm of Perot and Bissell (Fig. 6).

Changes in the roof line of the Winterthur house were made about 1884 while it was occupied by Colonel Henry Algernon du Pont.[10] The fenestration of the building was not basically altered, but a steep roof with large dormer windows and prominent brick chimneys was added—presumably to give the house a then more fashionable late-medieval appearance (Figs. 7, 8). Although it has not been possible to prove that Theophilus Chandler was responsible for this design, it is probable that he was since he handled other contracts for the Colonel's father; and similar houses attributed to him, such as the Silas Wright Pettit residence, State Road,

---

[10] Letter from H. F. du Pont to C. O. Cornelius, January 30, 1933. Winterthur Museum archives.

Fig. 7   North Facade of the Winterthur House,
photograph as the building appeared from 1884 to 1902.

Fig. 8   South Facade of the Winterthur House,
photograph as the building appeared from 1884 to 1902.

Fig. 9   North Facade of the Winterthur House,
photograph as the building appeared from 1903 to 1929.

Fig. 10   South Facade of the Winterthur House,
photograph as the building appeared from 1903 to 1929.

Bryn Mawr, Pennsylvania, bear strong resemblances to the remodeled Winterthur house.[11]

Between 1901 and 1903, many changes were made in Colonel du Pont's home, when the Philadelphia architectural firm of Robeson Lea Perot and Elliston Perot Bissell redesigned it in a modified Renaissance-revival style.[12] Throughout the second half of the nineteenth century it was generally believed that the Renaissance offered appropriate inspiration for distinguished houses, and it is understandable that an eclectic Renaissance style was chosen for the home of this prominent Delaware citizen. The new dormer windows were inspired by the architectural style of Francis I, a style which was much in favor for private homes in America at the turn of the century.[13] At this date, also, many buildings were designed with "melodious sky lines," or sky lines that were highly varied in their broken silhouette. Architects were interested in creating dominant and subordinate elements to give rhythm to their designs, and it is probably because of the popularity of this design theory that the Winterthur house first lost its original symmetrical arrangement (Fig. 1, 1903).

The most obvious exterior changes made between 1884 and 1903 are seen by comparing photographs of the north view of the building (Figs. 7 and 9). The old facade had been removed and a new one built with a porte-cochere in a late-Gothic style. The textured surface of the new tile roof contrasted vividly with the plain stucco walls below. Balconies were added on the third story, and a large window was set east of the entrance door to provide light for the main staircase. This staircase window was a conspicuous asymmetrical element foreign to the basic design of the earlier house. A hipped roof replaced the former peaked roof, and a balustrade was added at its top. The garden, or south side, of the building was least affected by the remodeling; but the old conservatory was refaced with stone, and a terrace wall was installed to raise the ground level a few feet (Fig. 10).

[11] See photograph of the Pettit residence, MOSES KING, *Philadelphia and Notable Philadelphians* (New York: Moses King, 1901), p. 90. Other buildings accredited to Chandler by King include the Pennsylvania Fire Insurance Company, 508 and 510 Walnut Street, Philadelphia; William Simpson, Jr., residence, "Ingeborg," Overbrook; William H. Joyce residence, Rosemont; Lincoln Godfrey residence, "Hillsover," Radnor and Chester Roads, Radnor (King, pp. 8B, 74, 81, and 82 respectively). The Pennsylvania Fire Insurance Company Building is discussed in detail by RICHARD G. CARROTT, "The Architect of the Pennsylvania Fire Insurance Building," *Journal of the Society of Architectural Historians,* XX (October, 1961), 138-139. According to Carrott, only three bays on the east side of the building were designed by Chandler. The west half of the building was designed by John Haviland in 1838.

[12] According to a statement made by Mr. Perot's third wife, he was born October 24, 1872, and died July 28, 1944. Mr. Perot was a graduate of the University of Pennsylvania, where he studied architecture. His drawings and papers relating to his profession have not been kept by his descendants, but it is known that he once worked for Mantle Fielding and that he designed many private residences and churches. Mr. Perot was a student of European architecture and had traveled abroad. For three years he was the president of the Germantown Historical Society and for forty-four years was the architect of the Germantown Academy, of which he was a board member. (Interview with Mrs. Robeson Lea Perot, July 27, 1963.)

Elliston Perot Bissell (b. November 23, 1872; d. July 3, 1944) was professionally associated with Mr. Perot for only a few years, when they had an office in the Philadelphia Bourse. Mr. Bissell graduated from the University of Pennsylvania in 1893, was a Fellow of the American Institute of Architects, and had a partnership with John P. B. Sinkler from 1907 to 1933. One of the works of this firm is the Confederate Memorial, known as Battle Abbey, in Richmond, Virginia. (Interview with Elliston Perot Bissell, Jr., July 29, 1963.)

[13] LOUIS H. GIBSON, *Beautiful Houses, A Study in House Building* (New York: Thomas Y. Crowell & Company, 1895), p. 159, states that the style of Francis I is decorative, exuberant, and "well suited to properly located American homes."

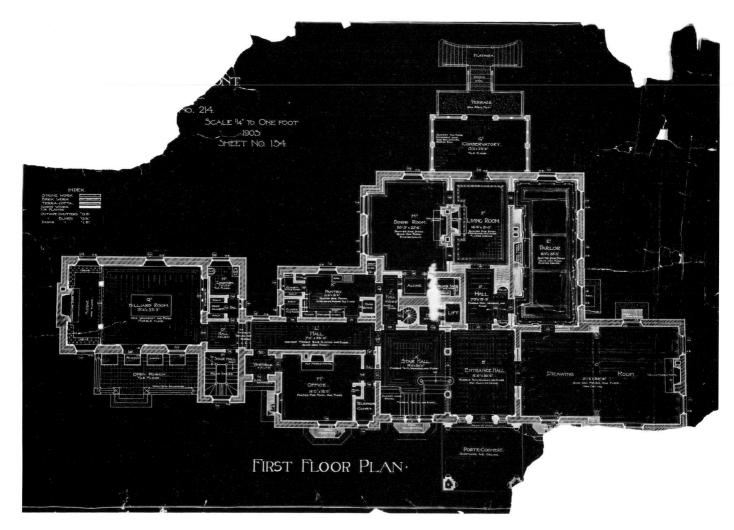

Fig. 11   Ground-Floor Plan of the Winterthur House, *blueprint by Perot and Bissell, dated 1903.*

The 1903 additions changed completely the ground-floor plan of the home (compare Fig. 6 with Fig. 11). The building was extended about 22 feet north of the original line to accommodate the new facade and the large entrance hall with trim, wainscot, and floor of marble. The dining room, living room, and parlor remained in relatively the same position, but were enlarged and refinished with painted pine paneling and Italian marble fireplaces. A large drawing room (21 by 39 feet) was added to the northwest where the Marlboro Room is now located, and on the east side were added an office, hall, and pantry. Beyond these, the building was further extended to the east to house areas for study and recreation—a squash court in the basement, a billiard room on the first floor, and a library on the second floor (Fig. 12).[14] The present Memorial Library at the Museum occupies the same space as the library designed by Messrs.

[14] The plans by Perot and Bissell were lent to this writer by Leslie P. Potts, general superintendent of Winterthur Farms.

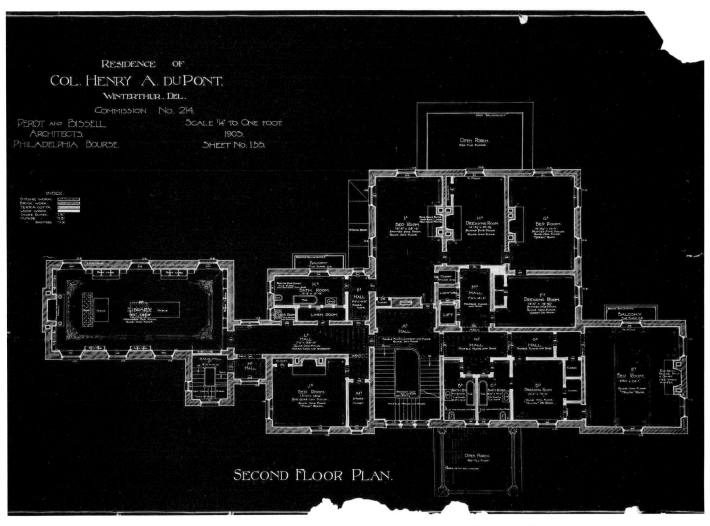

Fig. 12 Second-Floor Plan of the Winterthur House, *blueprint by Perot and Bissell, dated 1903.*

Perot and Bissell, while the squash court and billiard room have been converted into period installations.

In 1927, after Henry Francis du Pont inherited Winterthur from his father, the Wilmington architect, Albert Ely Ives, began drafting plans to accommodate Mr. du Pont's antique American interior woodwork.[15] Correspondence between Mr. Ives and Mr. du Pont is evidence that this development of the Winterthur house was no slight undertaking, since involved

---

[15] The following background on Mr. Ives is given by GEORGE S. KOYL (ed.), *American Architects Directory* (2d ed.; New York: R. R. Bowker Company, 1962), p. 341.

IVES, ALBERT ELY, AIA 35. Hawaii Chapter
    Albert Ely Ives, 1330 S. Beretania, Honolulu, Hawaii.
b. Newburgh, N. Y, July 10, 98. Educ: N. Y. Sch. of F. A, 18; N. Y. Sch. of F. A, Paris, 21. Dftsmn, Theodate Pape, 22; Delano & Aldrich, 25; Trainor & Fateo, 26; Addison Mizner, 28. Prev. Firms: Ives & Hogan. Present Firm: Albert Ely Ives, Archt, org. 55. Reg: Hawaii. Gen. Types: 1, 2, 5. Prin. Wks: Winterthur Mus, Wilmington, Del: Hana Mauai Hotel, T. Hawaii; Barbara Hutton, Cuernavaca, Mex, 59; S. F. B. Morse, Pebble Beach, Calif, 58; Honolulu Acad. of Arts, 61.

Fig. 13 North and West Facades of the Winterthur Museum,
photograph as the building appeared after 1930.

once again was the complete remodeling of the north façade, the dormer windows, roof, and interior areas (compare Figs. 9 and 13).[16] It was at this time, also, that the great expansion of the building was laid out which more than doubled the size of the original house and which, by replacing the conservatory on the south and extending down a hillside through the garden, created the modified T-shaped plan of the Winterthur Museum as it is seen today.

There were three basic parts to the extension of the Winterthur house made between 1928 and 1930. The schematic plan (Fig. 1, 1930) shows the first of these was a connecting passage between the old and new buildings in approximately the area where the conservatory had stood and where the Gamon Room is today. The second, and main addition, was rectangular in plan with a formal central hallway on the ground level—the Port Royal Entrance Hall.[17] This Georgian-period installation determined the exterior architectural character of the major section of the building (Fig. 14). The third section joined the main block at an obtuse angle; it was used as a service wing and secondary entrance. Photographs of the wing taken during its construction show views of the building (Figs. 15, 16) which are

---

[16] Correspondence between Henry Francis du Pont and Albert Ely Ives. Winterthur Museum archives.

[17] The Port Royal Entrance Hall and Parlor woodwork came from a house built in 1762 for Edward Stiles on Frankford Creek, near Philadelphia.

Fig. 14 Port Royal Entrance Portal of the Winterthur Museum,
photograph as the building appeared after 1930.

Fig. 15 Roof-Line Construction of the Winterthur House,
photograph dated 1930.

Fig. 16 Construction Southern Extension of the
Winterthur House, *photograph dated 1930.*

Fig. 17 View of the Winterthur Museum from the Southeast,
photograph as the building appeared from 1930 to 1946.

now obscured by still later additions. The extremely narrow height of the
1928-1930 extension, with its steeply pitched tile roof, gives the impression
that although early American buildings served as the basis for Mr. Ives's
design details, the scale of the remodeled Winterthur home was inspired
by European architecture.

The concept of creating a framework to accommodate interior woodwork from other buildings was not new in 1928, but it was somewhat of an
innovation in the field of the American decorative arts. The way in which
this was handled, to make the exterior of the Winterthur house compatible
with the interiors to be installed, resulted in extensive alterations to the
earlier part of the building and greatly changed its character. The Renaissance-revival façade was simplified to be more in keeping with the
Georgian elements introduced into the new addition; the old dormer windows were removed, and new ones, copied from those of the Port Royal

house, were substituted. Flat terra-cotta tiles replaced the earlier textured ones, and the roof-top balustrade was removed. Most important of all, the Port Royal Entrance on the west side became the main doorway to the house, and a new conservatory was built at the north facade, which had served as the formal entrance ever since the house was built.

From 1929 on, the Winterthur house became increasingly more inward-looking, with only isolated instances of early American architectural ornament added at vital points on the exterior, such as a doorway, a window, or a porch. For example, the columns, entablature, and pilasters of the Dining Room Porch (Fig. 17) were modeled after those of the giant porch of the Tuscan order on the south side of "The Woodlands," William Hamilton's country residence in West Philadelphia. The pilasters incorporated in the new conservatory were also adapted from "The Woodlands," but they were modeled after those of the north side of the Philadelphia mansion and are Ionic in style (Fig. 13).

Two different architectural approaches were involved in the growth of the house at Winterthur. Mr. Ives designed the framework and exterior, and to achieve a setting harmonious with the interior, modeled exterior elements after early American examples. Later, Thomas Waterman, a well-known American architectural historian and architect, provided plans for installing period woodwork and other interiors within the building.[18] However, it would be a mistake to infer that this type of architectural coordination took place throughout the building. Winterthur was a home, and many areas were not at first developed as period rooms. For example,

---

[18] Much of the following background on Thomas Waterman is adapted from an article written by HENRY FRANCIS DU PONT, "Thomas Tileston Waterman," *The Walpole Society Note Book* (The Walpole Society, 1952), pp. 35-37. During his youth, Thomas Tileston Waterman (b. East Orange, New Jersey, November 24, 1900; d. Washington, D. C., January 21, 1951) was a resident of New York City, where he attended Hamilton Grange and Berkley Schools. When about twenty years old, he began work with the Boston architectural firm of Cram and Ferguson, where he became Mr. Cram's private secretary and junior draftsman. A vital interest in early American architecture stimulated Waterman's activities in the Society for the Preservation of New England Antiquities, and he made measured drawings of the Province House prior to its razing. In 1928 Waterman studied abroad, making detailed drawings of the Cathedral at Palma, Island of Majorca. On return he was employed by the architectural firm of Perry, Shaw, & Hepburn in research and reconstructing the Governor's Palace and other buildings at Williamsburg. In 1933 Waterman headed the Historic American Buldings Survey and in 1940 turned to writing and private practice. He designed a hospital at the Marine Base, North Carolina, and performed research and restoration on many fine southern houses. Waterman was a designer and adviser for period installations at Winterthur from 1933 to 1950, during which time he was involved with many rooms, including the following: Marlboro Room, Lower Marlboro, Maryland, 1934; Patuxent Room, Lower Marlboro, Maryland, 1934; Montmorenci Stair Hall, Shocco Springs, North Carolina, 1936; Library Hall, Shocco Springs, North Carolina, 1936; Hart Room, Ipswich, Massachusetts, 1938; Queen Anne Dining Room, East Derry, New Hampshire, 1938; Blackwell Parlor, Philadelphia, Pennsylvania, 1939; Hardenbergh rooms, near Kerhonkson, New York, 1939-1940; Spatterware Hall, Wethersfield, Connecticut, and other rooms in the same area on eighth floor, 1939-1940; Morattico Hall and Flock Room, Richmond County, Virginia, 1940; Empire Hall, Shocco Springs, North Carolina, 1940-1941; Shop Lane and Court complex with woodwork ranging from Connecticut to North Carolina, 1946-1947; Oyster Bay Room, Oyster Bay, New York, 1947; Bertrand Room, Lancaster County, Virginia, 1947; Tappahannock Hall and Tappahannock Room, Essex County, Virginia, 1947.

Waterman was a member of the Walpole Society from 1947 to 1951 and wrote the following well-known books on American architecture: *Domestic Colonial Architecture of Tidewater, Virginia* (New York: C. Scribner's Sons, 1932); *The Early Architecture of North Carolina . . .* (Chapel Hill, N. C.: The University of North Carolina Press, 1941); *The Mansions of Virginia 1706-1776* (Chapel Hill, N. C.: The University of North Carolina Press, [1946]); *The Dwellings of Colonial America* (Chapel Hill, N. C.: The University of North Carolina Press, [1950]).

Fig. 18 Montmorenci Stair Hall.

only six years after the great extension of the building southward, Mr. du Pont replaced the Colonel's formal entrance stair hall with woodwork from Montmorenci, an early-nineteenth-century house near Warrenton, North Carolina. The installation was a remarkable feat of internal re-modeling, for it involved removing several large marble columns and a monumental marble staircase. Installed in place of the old staircase is a spiral wooden staircase from Montmorenci—a staircase that has become almost a symbol of Winterthur to most visitors (Fig. 18).

Another impressive space that required internal remodeling was the badminton court, originally designed by Ives, and redesigned in 1946 and 1947 by Thomas Waterman to accommodate architectural elements from actual facades, in full scale, of eighteenth- and early-nineteenth-century buildings. A comparison of photographs (Figs. 19, 20) shows the trans-formation that took place when the east side of the badminton court was adapted to a period setting with a facade of the Inn from Red Lion, Delaware.[19]

In planning the Court, Mr. du Pont was inspired to dramatize the decorative arts to give the viewer a true sense of the American heritage. Considering this goal and its achievement, the Court is, perhaps, the most imaginative and most emotionally moving setting at Winterthur. Photo-graphs fail to capture the mood of this great interior make-believe-out-of-doors setting, but one has only to visit the Court to know that Mr. du Pont's objective was handsomely realized. Twilight illumination leads the sensitive visitor to believe he is a part of the past. The controlled in-direct lighting and solitude offered by the Court induce a feeling which would be hard to achieve out of doors.[20]

In the Court, exterior architectural elements have been treated with the intimacy of an interior setting. This same effect was achieved by Thomas Waterman when he redesigned the bowling alleys and converted them to the late-eighteenth- and early-nineteenth-century Shop Lane, with store fronts from different parts of the Eastern Seaboard. This device of using exterior architectural elements in an interior setting is particularly effective in Shop Lane since it gives the visitor a feeling of openness that contrasts effectively with the more confined atmosphere of the adjoining period rooms.

In the same year that the Court and Shop Lane were installed, Leslie P. Potts, then assistant superintendent of Winterthur Farms, drew plans for a two-story addition to the southeast end of the Winterthur house (Fig. 1, 1946). The new section included a fan room, reception office, car-penter shop, and paint shop on the ground floor, and rooms for rug and curtain storage on the second. Most of these areas have since been adapted to other uses in later additions to the building.

No large exterior changes were made during the next few years while Mr. du Pont was turning his home and collections into a public museum

---

[19] One of the most recent installations at Winterthur is the facade, opposite the Red Lion Inn, from the Banister-MacKaye house near Newport, Rhode Island. The installation was completed in 1963 and, as in many other instances at Winterthur, this work preserved an example of early American architecture that soon would have been destroyed.

[20] No other diorama or stage set known to this writer gives the viewer such an opportunity to become a part of the scene. Charles F. Montgomery, former director of the Winterthur Museum, observed that the mood created by the Court is similar to that of Old Deerfield at dusk when the streets are empty.

Fig. 19 East Wall of Badminton Court in the Winterthur House,
photograph as the court appeared from 1930 to 1947.

Fig. 20   East Wall of Court Showing Part of Facade from Red Lion Inn,
photograph taken after 1947.

Fig. 21
South Wing of
Winterthur
Museum,
*photograph
taken 1959.*

and educational foundation. In 1956, however, Victorine and Samuel Homsey,[21] Wilmington architects, were asked to design a wing to house offices and an enlarged curtain storage room (Fig. 1, 1956), but this addition changed very little the basic appearance of the building; it merely extended the wing designed by Leslie Potts about 32 feet-farther east.

[21] Koyl, p. 323, gives the following background on Mr. and Mrs. Homsey:

HOMSEY, SAMUEL E(LDON). AIA 35, FAIA 54. Delaware Chapter

Victorine & Samuel Homsey, 2001 N. Scott St, Wilmington 6, Del.

b. Boston, Mass, Aug. 29, 04. Educ: MIT, B. S. & M. S, 26. Present Firm: Victorine & Samuel Homsey, Archts, org. 29. Reg: Del, Md, Mass, N. J, N. Y, Pa. Gen. Types: 1, 4, 5, 6, 7. Prin. Wks: Del. Art Ctr, Wilmington, & Res. for L. du P. Copeland, Greenville, 39; William W. M. Henry Comprehensive HS, Dover, 52; Frederick Douglass Stubbs Elem. Sch, W, 53; Off. Bldg, Winterthur Mus, Wilmington, & Experimental Greenhses. & Display Hses, Longwood Gardens, 59; all Del. Hon. Awards: 2 Hon. Men. Prizes, Gen. Motors Corp; Prize, Pittsburgh Glass Inst; Reg. & State Awards, Md. Soc. of Arch. Educ. Act: MIT Arch. Critic, 55: Nat. Arch. Accrediting Bd, 59. Pub. Serv: New Castle Co. Reg. Plan. Comm; Chmn, New Castle Co. Zoning Comm; Mem, Wilmington Bd. of Pks & Bd. of Penjerdel. Gov. Serv: U. S. N. R, 42-46. AIA Act: Del. Chapt; Pres, 52-53.

HOMSEY, VICTORINE DU PONT. AIA 44. Delaware Chapter

Victorine & Samuel Homsey, 2001 N. Scott St, Wilmington 6, Del.

b. Grosse Pointe, Mich, Nov. 27, 00. Educ: Wellesley Col, A. B, 23; Cambridge Sch. of Arch, M. Arch, 25. Present Firm: Victorine & Samuel Homsey, Archts, org. 29. Reg: Del. Gen. Types: 1, 4, 5, 6, 7. Prin. Wks: Del. Art Ctr, Wilmington, 39; Res. for L. du P. Copeland, Greenville, Del, 39: William W. M. Henry Comprehensive HS, Dover, Del, 52; Frederick Douglass Stubbs Elem. Sch, 53; Off. Bldg, Winterthur Mus, 59; Garden Tours Pavilion, W, 60. Hon. Awards: 2 Hon. Ment. Prizes, Gen. Motors Corp; Prize, Pittsburgh Glass Inst; Reg. & State Merit Awards, Md. Soc. of Archts. Gov. Serv: FPHA, 43-45.

While the period rooms and exterior walls of the Winterthur building have, since the Museum was opened, retained for the most part their former character, small additions and internal changes have been made and continue to be made. One of the more remarkable instances of internal remodeling took place in 1958, when wood and stonework from the Kershner farmhouse, near Reading, Pennsylvania, replaced the Pine Kitchen, a period installation which itself had replaced the working kitchen of the 1903 house. In order to preserve as far as possible the original dimensions of the Kershner Parlor, the east wall of the building at the ground level was moved about 1 foot out of plumb with the upper stories.

Six years after the Museum was opened, it was decided that still another addition was needed, and plans were drafted for a new wing to provide a meeting room for public lectures, a modern library, offices, maintenance shops, photographic studio, and improved guest reception and dining facilities.[22] Visitors arriving unaware that reservations must be made to see the period rooms in the Museum were often disappointed; so a series of installations which would give a capsule idea of the Winterthur collections and for which no appointment would be needed were a part of the plan for the new wing.

Since this was to be a large structure, it was important that it be visually harmonious with the main building, an effect which was achieved by Victorine and Samuel Homsey, who designed the seven-story addition (Fig. 21). The South Wing, as this addition is called, is highly varied in plan, for it serves many different functions. With the exception of the period rooms, all interior spaces are fitted with modern facilities and furniture. The exterior is businesslike in appearance, having a flat roof with an exposed elevator machine room covered with red terra-cotta tiles. The windows are capped with rusticated lintels modeled after those of the main structure. Antique architectural details incorporated in the South Wing are at the doorways and include the gates from the north side of the First Bank of the United States in Philadelphia at the Visitors' Entrance and, above this portal, the painted wooden lunette from a nineteenth-century building that once housed Philadelphia's Washington Hose Company (Fig. 22).[23] Another handsome doorway and porch is of the Federal period (Fig. 23), with woodwork from the front portico of "Oak Hill," a house built for Captain Nathaniel West and his wife, Elizabeth Derby West, near Peabody, Massachusetts. This doorway is used occasionally as an exit from the South Wing.

By September, 1959, preparations were being made to move the staff into its new quarters in the South Wing.[24] Woodwork in the period rooms was finished including some trim which had been salvaged from Mr. Bidermann's home when Colonel du Pont remodeled it in 1903. This early Winterthur woodwork was installed in Empire Hall, the last of the series of chronologically arranged rooms in the new addition (Fig. 24).

[22] Report of Charles F. Montgomery to the Directors of The Henry Francis du Pont Winterthur Museum, January 15, 1957, p. 6.

[23] CHARLES F. HUMMEL and M. ELINOR BETTS (eds.), *Philadelphia Reviewed: The Printmakers' Record 1750-1850, An Exhibition of Prints from the Collection of The Henry Francis du Pont Winterthur Museum* (Winterthur, Del., 1960), p. 42.

[24] Report to the Directors of The Henry Francis du Pont Winterthur Museum, September 21, 1959, p. 1.

Fig. 22
Painted Tympanum from
Washington Hose Company,
Philadelphia, *installed*
over main entrance,
South Wing.

Fig. 23
Portico from "Oak Hill,"
Peabody, Massachusetts,
after 1808, *installed on*
west facade South Wing.
Photograph taken in 1963.

Fig. 24 Empire Hall with Trim from Earliest Winterthur House,
installed in South Wing. Photograph taken in 1963.

Early in June, 1960, a feasibility study was completed for air conditioning all period rooms in the Winterthur Museum. This program, currently in progress, was undertaken for the preservation of objects in the collection by providing a relatively steady temperature level and humidity control. As a precaution against fire, the boilers for the heating plant were relocated outside the walls of the Museum, concealed in an underground equipment room in front of the west facade of the building. In this room are also housed the air-conditioning, humidity-control, air-filter, and water-circulation equipment. Tunnels have been dug around the building to carry the pipes and ducts necessary for air and water circulation, and an underground fan room has been constructed beneath the Conservatory. Refrigeration machinery is installed in a brick water tower that has stood since the nineteenth century in the gardens to the northwest of the Museum. The immense and complex task of installing the air-conditioning and new heating systems will, when completed, be a major step forward in the preservation of the collections.

In December, 1961, drawings were completed by Leon B. Musser for a connecting link across the low, gambrel-roofed buildings attached east of the South Wing (Fig. 1, 1962). This complex includes a terrace leading to the gardens, a receiving room, loading platform, rug and bedspread storage rooms, a fan room for the air-conditioning system, and a new period installation, the China Trade Room. The gambrel roof of the connecting building is covered with tile shingles that look like wood, and two of the original wooden dormer windows from the Port Royal house are incorporated in the east facade (Fig. 25). These, or similar dormers from the Port Royal house, had served as models for Albert Ely Ives when he designed the 1928-1930 addition to the Winterthur house.

In summary, it is oversimplification to say that the architectural evolution of the original Winterthur house can be traced from a relatively plain, symmetrical residence to the exceedingly complicated, asymmetrical home which has become the Museum. It is as difficult to make a general statement about the growth of the building as it is to gain a total visual impression of it from the ground. The Museum is so well suited to its surrounding gardens and sloping terrain that, large as the structure is, it cannot be seen in its entirety in the handsomely landscaped setting Mr. du Pont has created for it.

Although many designers have contributed their skills to planning the Winterthur house, the motivating force has always been Henry Francis du Pont; and the credit for achievement is his as the only person vitally concerned with the detailed changes made from the early part of this century to the present day. No man knows the history of the house better than Mr. du Pont, who has conceived and directed all the remodelings and additions undertaken since 1927. As organic architecture, the Museum is unique. Its form has been shaped by internal needs which have changed over the years; and its outward aspect has been dramatized by the imaginative arrangement of gardens and terraces, and by the preservation of old and noteworthy plantings, the locations of which have contributed in part to the asymmetrical form of the building. Like the chambered nautilus, Winterthur has steadily grown and changed from year to year; and, too, like the shell, its grand and relatively plain exterior only suggests in its outside design the beauty of the varied architecture composed within.

Fig. 25 Connecting Link Between Gambrel-Roofed Complex on the Southeast Side of the Winterthur Museum, *dormers from Port Royal mansion, c. 1762. Photograph taken in 1963.*

The Evolution of WINTERTHUR ROOMS

By JOHN A. H. SWEENEY

The Winterthur Museum is a collection and a house. There are many museums devoted to the decorative arts and many house museums, but rarely in America is a great collection displayed in a great country house. Passing through successive generations of a single family, Winterthur has been a private estate for more than a century. Even after the extensive renovations made to it between 1929 and 1931, the house remained a family residence. This fact is of importance to the atmosphere and effect of the Museum. The impression of a lived-in house is apparent to the visitor; the rooms look as if they were vacated only a short while ago—whether by the original owners of the furniture or by the most recent residents of the house can be a matter of personal interpretation. Winterthur remains, then, a house in which a collection of furniture and architectural elements has been assembled. Like an English country house, it is an organic structure; and the house, as well as the collection and the manner of displaying it to the visitor, has changed over the years. The changes have coincided with developing concepts of the American arts, increased knowledge on the part of collectors and students, and a progression toward the achievement of a historical effect in period-room displays. The rooms at Winterthur have followed this current, yet still have retained the character of a private house.

The concept of the period room as a display technique has developed gradually over the years in an effort to present works of art in a context that would show them to greater effect and would give them more meaning for the viewer. Comparable to the habitat group in a natural history museum, the period room presents the decorative arts in a lively and interesting manner, and provides an opportunity to assemble objects related by style, date, or place of manufacture. The difficulty in designing such installations is in determining the validity of the relationship of the objects. Do certain objects "go with" each other, or is their compatibility a factor imposed upon them by the knowledge and taste of the curators or collectors creating a period-room display? The answer to this question is difficult to determine, and it, too, has undergone a number of changes as the concept of the period room has emerged. In growing over the past forty years, the Winterthur collection has paralleled the development of the period room.

Joseph Downs wrote that the period room was best suited to the display of American decorative arts with their varied origins, materials, and dates and that regional differences, a factor of particular interest in the American arts, might be emphasized through this use of small units.[1] The American Wing of the Metropolitan Museum of Art pioneered in this type of display, attempting to provide a sympathetic and appropriate background for American furniture with woodwork and other architectural elements contemporary with it; but shortly after its opening, Homer Eaton Keyes, then editor of *Antiques,* raised two significant questions with regard to the installations. He doubted the "relative correctness of proportion" in a room where certain objects were installed—perhaps in greater number than would have been there originally—because the more appropriate objects were not available; and he wondered about the use of complete or partial reproductions of early American rooms to augment "those examples of the early home-builder's art which chance circumstance had preserved intact to the present day."[2] In answering his own questions, Keyes indicated the evolutionary nature of period-room displays and insisted upon the process of refinement that has been an essential factor in the Winterthur collection and in the rooms in which it is displayed:

> . . . *All this care concerning backgrounds carries with it important responsibilities for finishing each picture with full regard for the value of even the minutest details. That is an accomplishment not immediately to be wrought. Such pictures, like all thoughtful works of art, grow slowly. In the end they frequently owe less to initial inspiration than to an infinitude of patient correction.*[3]

In speaking of the changes made at Winterthur, Henry Francis du Pont reflected this concept when he remarked that "period rooms, which have never been plentiful, were bought as they came on the market and were reconstructed as nearly as possible in their original form; but it has taken all these years to get all the correct furniture and period rooms we needed, and needless to say every time a paneled room or mantelpiece was installed, I moved to this room the furniture that best suited it."[4] The rooms at Winterthur can be considered to have evolved, anticipating the discovery of new information or the availability of the perfect piece which would contribute to what Keyes thought of as the "picture" in a period room. It is desirable for a period room to contain woodwork of a specific place and date, reconstructed as nearly as possible in its original form, and for the furniture in it to be of the same region and period in order to achieve historical consistency. The Winterthur rooms have developed in this direction;

[1] Joseph Downs, "The History of the American Wing," *Antiques,* L (October, 1946), 233.

[2] Homer Eaton Keyes, "The Editor's Attic," *Antiques,* VII (April, 1925), 182.

[3] *Ibid.*

[4] Henry Francis du Pont, Letter to author, July 29, 1963.

the development is illustrated by recent photographs of the rooms compared with pictures taken of the same rooms in the 1930's.

The basic importance of the period-room installation was recognized by three students of Americana—Chauncey C. Nash, William D. Miller, and Norman M. Isham—after a visit to Winterthur reported in *The Walpole Society Note Book* for 1932:

> *The visit to Mr. du Pont's house, on Saturday, was something unique in Walpole experience. That group of peripatetics has seen many Early American rooms in many places. . . . All kinds have we passed through in museum after museum, but they were all rooms—museum rooms, silent places with polished floors, filled with polished, silent furniture standing in polite but aristocratic aloofness. Study and admiration they invite, intimacy is impossible. . . .*
>
> *We have seen restored houses, beautifully done, like that of Mr. Perry, or new houses like Mr. Palmer's, both unforgettably delightful as homes. Yet never have we seen so many old American rooms under one roof. . . . Nor could we imagine that there could be put into one house so many rooms so different, in size,*

period and character, in such way as to make it liveable—to make a home of it. But Mr. du Pont has done it. Here are rooms that welcome the guest, furniture which seems glad to receive him. There is nothing of the museum in the air. We are not among the dead.[5]

Placing antique furniture, paintings, and other decorative objects in such a context achieved a definite and desired effect. Writing in the same publication of the Walpole Society, the late Luke Vincent Lockwood described the appearance of one of the rooms at Winterthur as "a great comfortable room on the mezzanine floor furnished with the substantial, dignified, simple, oak and pine furniture of our early years."[6] Lockwood thus conceptualized the atmosphere of seventeenth-century America, and a photograph of the Wentworth Room as it appeared in 1935 (Fig. 1) suggests the impression it had made upon this distinguished collector and writer. He went on to describe the room:

Two cupboards, open below, our rarest type, a chest of drawers, the carving picked out in color, three seventeenth century washstands. Connecticut chest and chairs and tables of the period. The silver represents examples of all the best known early silversmiths and the three painted panels in their original frames are unique. On the floor is a splendid seventeenth century Asia Minor rug such as are occasionally mentioned in our inventories.[7]

The furniture described has since been relocated in other rooms of the Museum. Coming from a seventeenth-century New Hampshire house remodeled about 1710, the Wentworth Room was for a number of years the earliest room at Winterthur; and all the seventeenth-century furniture in the collection was originally placed there. When a room from the Thomas Hart house, built about 1670 in Ipswich, Massachusetts, was installed in 1938, the court cupboard shown against the far wall in the photograph was moved to that room. The court cupboard has a history of ownership in Ipswich and is attributed to the master joiner Thomas Dennis, who worked in that town in the late seventeenth century. It is, therefore, in a more appropriate setting. The chest of drawers, its "carving picked out in color," is also attributed to Thomas Dennis and is a remarkable example of seventeenth-century painted furniture. It is now installed in the Oyster Bay Room, next to the Hart Room, and it relates to seventeenth-century furniture of a similar type grouped with it. The long panel painting above the court cupboard now forms part of the fireplace wall in the Flock Room, where it is reunited with the woodwork from the house in which it was originally used. The restoration of this panel to its framework (from Morattico in Richmond County, Virginia), discovered and acquired for Winterthur ten years later, is a remarkable example of architectural reconstruction. The resulting Flock Room was described by Thomas T. Waterman, who supervised its installation, as "the finest of its type in Virginia, if not in the country."[8]

[5] "The Meeting at Winterthur," *The Walpole Society Note Book* (privately printed, 1932), p. 26.
[6] *Ibid.,* p. 22.
[7] *Ibid.*
[8] Thomas T. Waterman, *The Mansions of Virginia 1706-1776* (Chapel Hill, N. C.: The University of North Carolina Press, 1945), p. 62.

Fig. 2
China Hall, *Winterthur,*
photograph dated 1935.

Through the years, other rooms in the Museum have changed in a similar manner. In some cases the objects displayed have been adjusted or replaced as others have been acquired; in other rooms the architectural setting has been revised. China Hall (Fig. 2), as shown in 1935, contained a large service of Chinese export porcelain ordered by George Washington in 1785 for his own use and ornamented with the arms of the Society of the Cincinnati. The service was displayed in tall cupboards framed by moldings and carved lintels which repeat details in the woodwork of the adjacent Chinese Parlor. In front of the cupboards were Philadelphia side chairs made about 1760. They combine features of the Queen Anne and Chippendale styles and are appropriate to the bold moldings of the woodwork. About 1940 the architectural details in the China Hall were removed, and the doorway was replaced with late-eighteenth-century reeded trim ornamented with plaster composition figures, from a house in Georgetown, District of Columbia (Fig. 3). Matching trim frames the window. The woodwork is contemporary with the porcelain and is closely related to it by its neoclassical decoration. The shelves have been replaced by arched cupboards designed by Waterman to complement the woodwork. The furnishings of the hall have also changed. Replacing the Chippendale chairs are a window seat and side chair made in Salem, Massachusetts, about 1795 and probably carved by Samuel McIntire, the master carver of that seaport city. A richly embroidered mull curtain hangs at the window,

Fig. 3 China Hall, *woodwork from a house in Georgetown, District of Columbia, 1790-1800, photograph made in 1962.*

draped in a manner suggested by engravings and design-book illustrations of the late eighteenth and early nineteenth centuries.

The Chestertown Room contains woodwork from a house built about 1762 on Water Street in Chestertown, Maryland. Its architectural interest is derived from such features as the sunk panels on the wall, dentil cornice, pedimented overmantel, and mahogany cap above the fret-carved chair rail. In 1935 (Fig. 4) the room was furnished primarily with important pieces of Philadelphia Chippendale furniture. A rare easy chair, displaying carved arm terminals and a scalloped mahogany skirt above cabriole legs, stands beside the fireplace. A Philadelphia side chair is in the window recess, and another one stands next to the easy chair; a historic American looking glass hangs above a New York Chippendale card table. Because the date of the woodwork coincides with that of the high point of the Chippendale style in Philadelphia and because the architecture is similar to that fashionable in Philadelphia at that time, the furnishings shown here are entirely appropriate. Two factors contributed to a change in the furnishings of this room. Over the years there has come into the Winterthur collection an important group of furniture made in Newport, Rhode Island. An urn stand, attributed to the shop of John Townsend, stood next to the

Fig. 5   Chestertown Room, *Winterthur, photograph made in 1960.*

easy chair in the 1935 view of the Chestertown Room. Since then, it has been joined by other pieces of furniture made in Newport (Fig. 5), including a drop-leaf breakfast table labeled by John Townsend, a block-front chest of drawers, a straight-legged card table, and two mahogany tea tables, one of which is documented to the shop of John Goddard. Still hanging on the wall at the right is the looking glass given by Martha Washington in 1795 to the wife of John E. Van Alen, congressman from Rensselaer County, New York. That the pieces of furniture are from the

same city—some of them even from the same workshop—is an important coincidence which makes it possible for the student to study the characteristic features of a related group of objects. Here, the change in furnishings has also involved a process of bringing together pieces of a scale appropriate to the proportions of the architecture, a process which might be termed purely aesthetic, aimed at improving the visual effect of the room. A fact of interest to the student of American history is that the Newport cabinetmakers engaged in a lucrative export trade to cities along the eastern seacoast. The little port of Chestertown on Maryland's Eastern Shore was among those to which ships brought pottery and furniture from Rhode Island, and thus it is possible that Newport furniture might have been in a Maryland room. A few examples have been recovered in the South. In 1938 the elaborately carved woodwork from the parlor of the Blackwell house on Pine Street in Philadelphia was installed at Winterthur, and the Philadelphia furniture which had been in the Chestertown Room was moved to the new room, where the relationship of the architecture to the furniture is dramatically obvious.

Changes in the Baltimore Drawing Room (Fig. 6), used as a morning room before Winterthur became a museum, indicate a development toward

Fig. 7 Baltimore Drawing Room, *Winterthur, photograph made in 1960.*

a greater concentration of furniture from one region. The physical arrangement of the room is similar to that of the front rooms of Baltimore town houses built at the turn of the nineteenth century, with windows on the long wall facing the street and the fireplace on the wall at right angles to it. The mantelpiece is decorated with plaster composition ornament probably made at the factory of Robert Wellford in Philadelphia; similar examples of plaster ornament appear in Baltimore houses. In 1935 Baltimore card tables flanked the projecting chimney breast. A mahogany and satinwood desk characteristic of Baltimore stood at the left of the window, and Baltimore side chairs were to be seen in the room. A New England sofa, probably made in Salem, Massachusetts, was at the right of the fireplace; it faced a Connecticut or New York upholstered armchair, beside which was a satinwood sewing table from Philadelphia. These objects have been moved. Replacing the Baltimore card tables are unusual marble-topped corner stands decorated in a manner peculiar to Baltimore (Fig. 7).

Fig. 8
Dancing Room, *woodwork*
from Ritchie house,
Tappahannock, Virginia,
before 1725, Winterthur,
photograph dated 1935.

Where the Martha Washington chair stood, there is now a Baltimore sofa with a curved back and tapered legs inlaid with satinwood bellflowers typical of Baltimore design. A small Baltimore urn stand is beside it. The same Baltimore side chairs flank the desk. The consistent factors in the room, such as the carpet, the curtains, and the pictures on the wall, suggest the ability of such objects to be used sympathetically with various furnishings. While these particular items do not have histories of ownership in Baltimore, they are presumably similar to things available in Baltimore at the time that the furniture was made. Their use demonstrates the important practice in period-room display of including examples of the lesser household equipment that give the room a lifelike quality.

When Winterthur was enlarged in 1929, paneling from an early house in Virginia (the Ritchie house at Tappahannock) was used to line the walls of the Dancing Room (Fig. 8). This provided a pleasing background for Windsor chairs, early-eighteenth-century tables, hooked rugs, and nineteenth-century pottery. The spirit of the room conveyed the direct charm and simplicity usually associated with early American life, and a period-room display was not attempted. Subsequently the room was revised completely and the woodwork installed as it was believed to have been in the

Fig. 9 Tappahannock Room, *Winterthur, photograph made in 1950.*

house in Tappahannock (Fig. 9). When the Walpoleans visited Winterthur again in 1948, Thomas T. Waterman described the change: "In
deference to their great importance as among the oldest of Virginia paneled
rooms du Pont had them reconstructed last year, in exact accordance with

Fig. 10 Court, *Port Royal Facade composed of architectural elements from Port Royal, Frankford, Pennsylvania, 1762, photograph made in 1950.*

Fig. 11 Court, *Banister Facade, from Banister-MacKaye house, Middletown, Rhode Island, 1756, photograph made in 1963.*

their original state. The hall room has one wall plastered as of old, but this is now covered by a painted cloth wall covering, with a soft green background."[9] Originally a parlor and hall, or passage, the two rooms are now installed side by side rather than as one large irregularly shaped room; and the furniture in the room has been adjusted to include objects made in the Middle Colonies in the second quarter of the eighteenth century, approximately contemporary with the woodwork. Such a revision marks a move on the part of the collector to bring into alignment the architecture and furnishings of a room. Rather than the woodwork's being utilized merely as the background and unifying factor in the display of the collection, the two are coordinated in an ensemble which has a specific meaning of its own.

At about the time that the change was made in the Tappahannock rooms, an interior badminton court was turned into a courtyard designed by Waterman "not only to display a collection of outdoor furniture, but architectural fragments as well."[10] The walls of this interior space were faced with house fronts, one of which simulated the exterior of Port Royal, built in 1762 at Frankford, Pennsylvania, from which a number of interiors at Winterthur had come (Fig. 10). Waterman described it as "stuccoed as so many Philadelphia houses were. . . . The west wall, then, is in the Philadelphia style of, say, 1765-1775 and forms a setting for a beautifully designed and worked Doric doorway."[11] In 1959 the doorway was removed for use as a new entrance to the Museum. The entire facade was later replaced by the actual rusticated wooden exterior of the Banister-MacKaye house, built in 1756 near Newport, Rhode Island (Fig. 11); and thus the adjustment continues. In this instance a display, which was not part of a conventional domestic setting for a collection of antiques and which had more of an educational character than the earlier installations, was replaced in time by an actual house front which "chance circumstance had preserved" and which also illustrated an important aspect of American architectural history.

As an evolving setting, Winterthur reveals the growth of a collection and the development of the interests and tastes of the collector in the course of the process described by Homer Eaton Keyes as the "infinitude of patient correction." Mr. du Pont has said that he wanted his collection to show Americans how Americans have lived and that to this end he bought every period of furniture and interior architecture between 1640 and 1830 that could be accommodated in his house. With the purpose of utilizing a collection of the decorative arts to demonstrate history, the arrangement of the objects passes beyond the furnishing of a house and takes into consideration historical and anthropological factors. The period room is suited to such a purpose, and at the same time provides a setting which shows to advantage the objects made by, used by, and available to early Americans. As the knowledge of the Americans and their arts increase, and as the hoped-for perfect pieces become available, these settings are bound to change. In so doing they reflect the dynamic qualities of the collector and the collection.

[9] "Pilgrimage to Winterthur and Hunting Hill," *The Walpole Society Note Book* (privately printed, 1948), p. 52.
[10] *Ibid.*, p. 49.
[11] *Ibid.*, p. 50.

Fig. 12 Williams Room, *from Welles-Williams house, Lebanon, Connecticut, circa 1725.*

Illustrative of the continuing process of "patient correction" is the Williams Room, formerly the Belle Isle Room, where recent revisions have resulted in a closer relationship between the architecture and furniture. Since the 1929-31 renovations, New England furniture had been displayed in a room from Belle Isle, a plantation house in Lancaster County, Virginia; but it is now arranged in a room which is somewhat smaller, has a lower ceiling, and is of a scale more appropriate to it. In place of the Virginia woodwork, grained and marbleized paneling from the early-eighteenth-century Welles-Williams house at Lebanon, Connecticut, which became available in 1959, adds to the Museum an outstanding example of decorated interior architecture. Next to the blocked fireplace opening is a New England easy chair upholstered in flame-stitch wool embroidery. An early Connecticut maple day bed faces it; at the left are chairs attributed to the shop of John Gaines in Portsmouth, New Hampshire. The moldings of the Connecticut desk and bookcase are painted black in contrast to the cherry wood case. Much of the furniture in the room, including the rare splay-legged table, is related stylistically through the appearance of brush-shaped Spanish feet. The boldness of the paneling and moldings, as well as the imaginatively painted surfaces, complements the direct simplicity of the New England furniture; and the ensemble presents a charming and effective image of a rural Connecticut room dating from before 1750.

The History and Development
of the
WINTERTHUR GARDENS

By C. GORDON TYRRELL

The Winterthur Estate came into existence in 1839 when James Antoine Bidermann and his wife, Evelina Gabrielle, the daughter of E. I. du Pont de Nemours, built their home (Fig. 1) on the present site of the museum and named it "Winterthur," after the town in Switzerland where Mr. Bidermann's family had lived. The gardens, which today comprise some forty acres of the estate's eleven hundred, had their origin in a sunken garden laid out by the Bidermanns near their new home. At the back of the original square house was a porch which was glassed in during the winter and used as a conservatory. Below this was a sloping lawn going down to the road which today passes the south wing entrance of the museum. On one side of the lawn was a big tulip poplar, and on the other were two hemlocks as well as a large Norway spruce, which was cut down when the dining room wing was added. Today, the museum occupies this whole area. However, the tulip poplar, covered with ivy, still stands to the east of the museum, and the two hemlocks ennoble the Port Royal entrance. They are huge trees now.

At the bottom of the hill, just beyond the service entrance, stands the old crab-apple *(Malus scheideckeri)* which was planted by Mr. Bidermann. *Aesculus parviflora* and other shrubs were planted in the area adjacent to the crab-apple and along the meadow which ran to the stream beyond.

*Fig. 1 Original Bidermann house showing cold frames and vegetable garden.
Reproduced by permission of the Eleutherian Mills Historical Library.*

The Bidermanns' sunken garden, containing a greenhouse, was in the area that comprises the museum guest parking lot today (Fig. 2-S). Immediately above this garden, on the site of the present swimming pool and its small garden, were a larger greenhouse, cold pits, and garden service area which provided flowers and vegetables for the house. In 1902, when the house was owned by Colonel Henry A. du Pont, a nephew of Mrs. Bidermann, the library wing was being added to the house and the greenhouses were transferred to their present site (Fig. 2-B). In their place were developed a small pool and two garden houses with an arbor-covered wall fountain between them. This then became the upper terrace of the garden. The two lower terraces, which comprised the area of the Bidermanns' sunken garden, were separated by three arbors of wisteria. One of these terraces was devoted to lawn and wide herbaceous borders of delphinium, poppies, peonies, foxgloves, and similar plantings, with a few pear trees for their flowering effect (Fig. 3); the other was a rose garden, with a lily pool at its east end and a fence separating the whole area from the meadow. This lower level was the favorite of Mr. H. F. du Pont's mother, and judging from colored slides, it was indeed a lovely garden. It was destroyed in the name of progress in 1957, when the parking lot was developed. All that remains to be seen of it today are the three

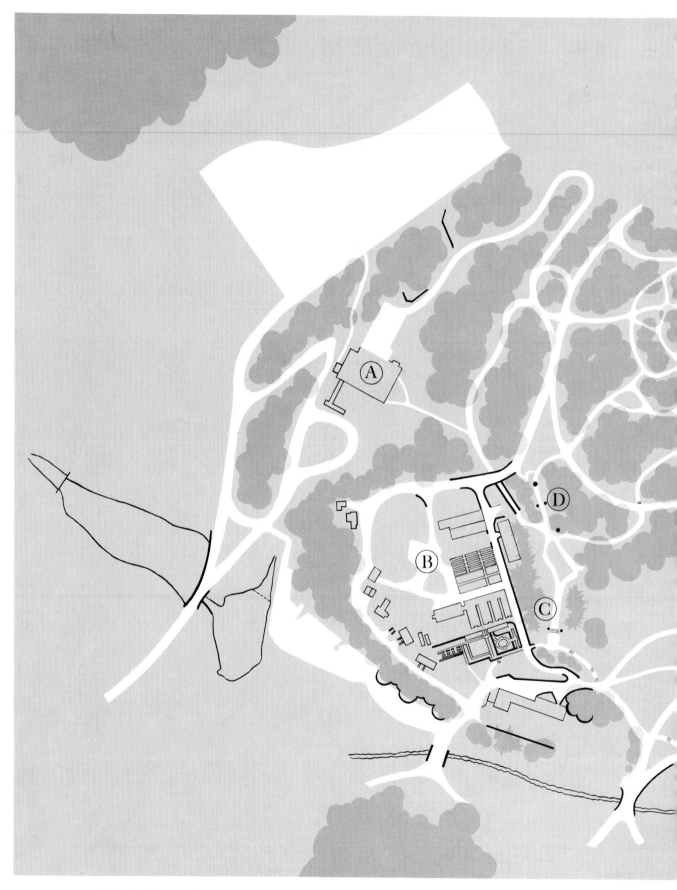

Fig. 2 Map of Winterthur Gardens.

KEY TO MAP OF WINTERTHUR GARDENS

A. The Pavilion.
B. Site of the Present Greenhouses.
C. Site of the Old Iris Garden
   and the Present Saunders Peony Garden.
D. George and Martha Washington.
E. The Azalea Woods.
F. The March Walk.
G. The Saucer Magnolias.
H. The White Kurume Azaleas and Dogwood.
I. The Old Path to the Sundial Garden.
J. The Corylopsis-Mucronulatum Walk.

K. The Pinetum.
L. The Chaenomeles Walk and Viburnums.
M. The Sundial Garden.
N. The White Gate.
O. The Lookout.
P. The Sycamore Area and Bristol Summerhouse.
Q. The Primula Quarry.
R. Oak Hill.
S. The Present Museum Parking Lot
   and Site of Original Sunken Garden.
T. The Goldfish Pond and Waterfalls.
★ The Cedar Atlantica Glauca Circle.

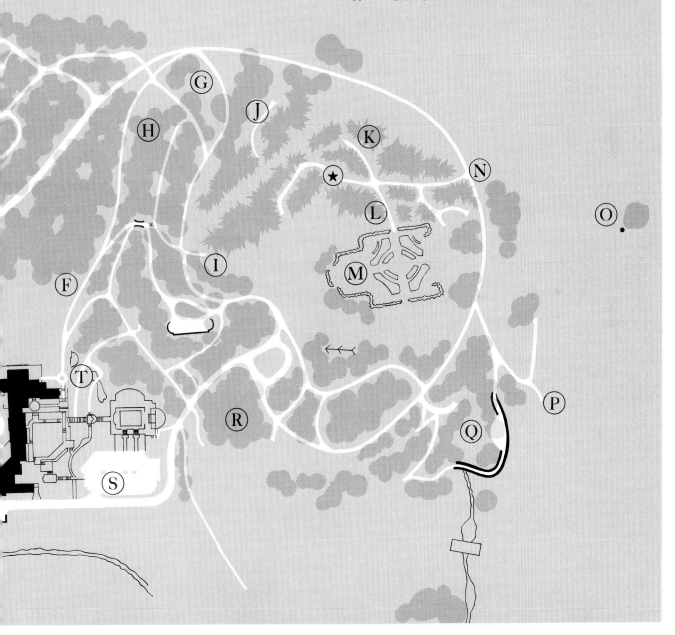

*Fig. 3 View from the museum terrace showing the lower
section of the sunken garden and the meadows beyond, c. 1950.*

arbors with wisteria, which are in their original positions, and the arbor-
covered wall fountain, which is against the east wall.

Prior to 1931, the front door of the house was situated where the
conservatory is today, and was approached via the drive from the present
Peony Steps. Before the greenhouses were moved, this road swung around
and down through the valley east and below the house (Fig. 4) just beyond
the upper fish pool, passing between the present garden gates and the hillside with the big beech at the left, and meeting the drive at about the present
parking space entrance. The woods at the front of the old house had by
then been cleared and made into lawn, and in 1902 Mr. Henry F. du Pont
began naturalizing daffodils along its edge. Most of these plants still bloom
in the "Narcissus Grove" today (Fig. 5). Planting of the adjacent March
Bank was also started at this time (Fig. 4). By 1910 there were grape-
hyacinths, snowdrops, squills, chionodoxa, iris, dwarf daffodils, crocus,

Fig. 4   *House and driveway before 1931, also showing March Walk.*

Fig. 5   *Front of the old house with part of the "Narcissus Grove."*

adonis, and other small bulbs blooming there. At the far end of the March Walk, extending from the front of the old house to the bend in the back drive, were the saucer magnolias which had been planted at an early date by Colonel du Pont. These trees, which have attained a massive size, are today one of the most striking displays in the garden (Fig. 2-G).

When the greenhouses were relocated in 1902 to their present position, only the potting shed and three houses were erected: the present orchid house, rose house, and geranium house. The sunken gardens below the greenhouses, which today contain a collection of peonies, columbine, astilbe, and other perennials, were developed at this time. Colored slides taken in 1910 and 1911 show the border of colorful perennials, with some particularly fine delphinium against the high wall on the side towards the greenhouse.

Thus by 1910 we find in existence a small swimming pool, a lovely formal garden with roses and many other plants, a greenhouse area with an excellent perennial garden attached, a portion of woodland planted with daffodils and other bulbs, and many choice shrubs and trees planted in various areas of the garden.

Between 1912 and 1915 many fine new plants from Japan were exhibited at the San Francisco World's Fair. Among them were the Kurume azaleas, which before this date had never been seen in the United States. Some of these plants later found their way to various nurseries in this country, and in 1914 Mr. H. F. du Pont happened to spot and obtain seventeen plants from the Cottage Garden Nurseries on Long Island. These were bought out of flower, as varieties that the florists did not think would be suitable for forcing, and became the nucleus of the extensive plantings of Kurume azaleas in the Azalea Woods—plantings of delicate shades and colors, and combinations that go together with no trouble at all (Fig. 2-E). It is amazing that from this shot in the dark, as it were, so much beauty has evolved.

Mr. H. F. du Pont's gardener, Robertson, taking cuttings from these seventeen plants, began to build a small nursery area from which, by 1920, it was possible to start developing the Azalea Woods. Until this time the oaks and tulip poplars shared the woods with the American chestnut. The chestnut blight, however, by 1911 had spread through Pennsylvania and adjacent states, and in a short time the trees at Winterthur were fatally stricken. The removal of these giant trees from the woodland left large open areas which, in the Azalea Woods, were subsequently filled with the newly-propagated Kurume azaleas (Fig. 6).

Besides the Kurumes, there are a few other groups of azaleas which came to Winterthur during those early years. *Rhododendron schlippenbachi,* the Royal Azalea, and *R. kaempferi,* the Torch Azalea, were both sent to Mr. H. F. du Pont in 1919 by Prof. Charles Sprague Sargent, the first director of the Arnold Arboretum. Today, the royal azalea opens its soft pink flowers over a large portion of the Pinetum, and the torch azalea is one of the dominant features of the Azalea Woods.

We can only speculate as to the origin of the so-called "late kaempferi hybrid" azaleas, which seem to be unique to Winterthur and which Paul Bosley, an azalea specialist, years ago dubbed the "Winterthur Azaleas." Though it was certainly very early, it is not known just when they came, nor is their originator or exact parentage known. Research done years

Fig. 6   Azalea Woods showing the tall tulip poplars, dogwoods, and Kurume azaleas.

ago by Mr. H. F. du Pont indicates that they may have come from the hand of Charles Sander, gardener to Prof. Sargent at his estate in Brookline, Massachusetts. As early as 1885, Mr. Sander was hybridizing forcing-azaleas, and it seems probable that with later introductions of hardier species he might have attempted to produce hybrids which would survive out of doors.

One other azalea remains to be accounted for: the beautiful *R. mucronatum* 'Magnifica.' Today this is probably the most widely-used azalea cultivar in the whole garden and one, incidentally, which visitors never fail to ask about. It has a clear lavender-mauve mutation which arose here and was named 'Winterthur.' This sport has the added distinction of being deliciously fragrant, something quite unusual in oriental azaleas. Though it is quite certain that 'Magnifica' came to Winterthur very early, its source and the exact date of its arrival are not known. *R. mucronatum* and its forms were introduced from the Orient at an earlier date than the

Kurumes *(R. mucronatum* itself being brought from China to England as early as 1819), so it seems reasonable to assume that our plants of 'Magnifica' have been at Winterthur for a long time.

Colonel and Mr. H. F. du Pont were in Europe in 1914, sailing home when war was declared in August. Shortly after his arrival home, the Colonel began laying out the collection of conifers known today as the Pinetum (Fig. 2-K). More than fifty species and varieties of fir, spruce, hemlock, arbor-vitae, juniper, false-cypress, cedar, and pine were put in, and the collection today is substantially the same as it was in the beginning —except the trees are now fine, tall specimens. Over the years there has been the inevitable small percentage of losses, but the only additions to the original planting have been two trees of the Dawn Redwood *(Metasequoia glyptostroboides),* planted by Mr. H. F. du Pont in 1951 and 1957. The dawn redwood was first discovered in 1945 in the remote interior of China. In 1948 viable seed was obtained by the Arnold Arboretum, and it is likely that our larger tree came from this original seed lot. Known only by fossil remains prior to this time, the species is estimated to be fifty million years old. Quite ornamental in appearance, it has a tremendous rate of growth; though no more than fifteen years old, the larger tree at Winterthur is already as tall as the surrounding fifty-year-old conifers.

Mention might be made of some of the trees planted in 1914 by Colonel du Pont which today are dominant features in the Pinetum. Easily the most striking of these is the Blue Atlas Cedar *(Cedrus atlantica glauca),* which is one of the most beautiful trees in the world. There are two in the Pinetum—both tall, broad, mature trees—with their graceful habit and silvery-blue foliage creating a splendid effect at all seasons of the year. Another conifer of extraordinary beauty is the Japanese Umbrella-pine *(Sciadopitys verticillata),* distinguished also for its rarity and slow rate of growth. The two at Winterthur, both tall, well-furnished specimens, are as fine as any in this country. Not so rare, but an excellent tree, is the Oriental Spruce *(Picea orientalis),* one of the finest of all the spruces. There are several of these lining the walks and forming backgrounds for the many bright shrubs in the Pinetum. Their tall, dark spires, together with the deep green columns of the equally fine *Libocedrus decurrens,* the Incense-cedar, are one of the most attractive sights in that area of the garden.

There were many choice trees and shrubs at Winterthur by the time of the First World War—among them buckeyes, tree peonies, azaleas and rhododendrons, honey-suckle, weigela, Japanese maple, witch-hazel, wisteria, forsythia, clematis, magnolias, lilacs, crab-apples, and cherries. One of the most notable of these was the rare Chinese *Davidia involucrata,* the Dove Tree. Mr. H. F. du Pont first purchased this tree from the famous Veitch nurseries in England in 1902. In 1924 Prof. Sargent wrote that he knew of only three plants of Davidia in the whole country—one at the Arnold Arboretum, one belonging to a Mrs. Gibbs, and one at Winterthur. He added also that the tree at Winterthur was the best-looking specimen of the lot. This same tree flourishes today along the walk from the museum terrace, just beyond the service entrance of the south wing. In more recent times another specimen was acquired. This has now reached large size, and in 1961 was moved from the nursery to the area of the Sycamore. Even today, the dove tree is seldom seen in American gardens.

The development of the garden has always been closely tied to extension of the house, and the next era of garden history coincides with the great addition to the house during the years 1929-31. At that time, much work was done on the terraces and other features of the garden to the east of the museum. On the site of the small pool with the two garden houses which was built in 1902, the present swimming pool was constructed. In 1935 ornamental grillwork from the newly-arrived Montmorenci Stair Hall was used on top of the wall around the swimming pool. Beginning about 1930, on the bank below the caddy space east of the library wing, Miss Marian Coffin and the Mayfair Nurseries created a series of small water-falls and the goldfish pond below them (Fig. 2-T). Now turned on only when required, these falls originally tumbled down the slope among the rocks to the pool below. The bills of thirty-three years ago reveal that 375 perennials were used here, ten of each kind. Of these, the only survivor is *Corydalis cheilanthifolia,* which has seeded itself in the rocks.

Also in 1929 an iris garden was laid out in the area (Fig. 2-C) between the present Peony Steps and the figures of George and Martha Washington (Fig. 2-D). This was given up ten years later because it was found that iris enthusiasts were interested only in the newest varieties, and by the time enough of these had been propagated to make an effect, they were has-beens. After 1939 the area was planted with seedling Ghent azaleas. These remained until 1946, when they were moved to their present location on the path to the White Gate (Fig. 2-N); in their place were put azaleas 'Magnifica' and 'Coral Bells' which remain there today. At this time there were some peonies in the area below the greenhouse, but the Saunders Peony Garden as we know it now did not come into existence until after 1953. Today it holds a fine collection of Japanese, Chinese, and French hybrid peonies, with the dominant group being both tree and herba-ceous peonies of the Saunders strain. These were produced by the late Prof. A. P. Saunders of Clinton, New York, who brought together an unpar-alleled assemblage of peony species from all over the world and produced hybrids from them, the like of which had never before been seen. Introduc-tion of these hybrids has been relatively recent—a few in the 'thirties, many in the 'forties, and several in the 'fifties—but the Oriental and the French tree peonies are much older. In this garden are three plants of a deep purple form of *Paeonia suffruticosa,* the Chinese Moutan Peony, which have been at Winterthur since 1880, and also a few plants of the French hybrids (produced by M. Lemoine) 'La Lorraine' and 'Souvenir de Maxime Cornu' which were brought over in 1910 and 1925.

At this point it is appropriate to mention some of the garden orna-ments found in and around the Peony Garden. The hollow cast metal figures of George and Martha Washington (Fig. 7) on the path beyond the Peony Garden came to Winterthur via an unknown source in 1950. These are old-fashioned "stove tops"—ornamental figures which decorated the tops of the huge stoves found in homes many years ago, before the advent of steam heat. They served the very practical purpose of holding and dis-tributing heat in the room, a purpose often served less decoratively by a regular length of stovepipe, looped half-way across the room before connecting with the chimney flue. The figures of George and Martha Washington at Winterthur were originally produced at the Mott Iron

Fig. 7   George and Martha Washington with Azalea 'Magnifica.'

Works of New York,[1] which were in existence from 1823 to 1850. The summerhouse and "bee hives" in the Peony Garden, the roofed, circular garden seat, and the roofed archway beyond George and Martha all came in 1929 and 1930 from Miss Mary Latimer of Wilmington, as did the White Gate in the Pinetum. Miss Latimer was the niece of John Richardson Latimer, a China Trader, who purchased in 1838 an estate on Maryland Avenue in Wilmington, just beyond the southwest city line near the suburb now known as Richardson Park. This estate, which he called "Latimeria," dated from 1815 when it was built for Mr. William Warner. Mr. H. F. du Pont's great-grandfather, E. I. du Pont, designed the plans for the house.

In 1927, when Mr. H. F. du Pont took over the gardens on the death of his father, the first area he developed was the Pinetum (Fig. 2-K) and (Fig. 8), where paths were laid out through the conifers, and work was started on planting the Chaenomeles Walk and the groups of viburnums (Fig. 2-L) which we see there today. At this time too the bank of white

[1] "Riddles and Replies," *Antiques,* Vol. XLIII (January, 1943), 41.

Fig. 8   Section of the Pinetum with Azalea mucronata alba.

Kurume azaleas were planted in front of the dogwood along the west end of the Pinetum (Fig. 2-H). Directly opposite these azaleas was the Corylopsis-mucronulatum Walk (Fig. 2-J) which was planted sometime in the 'twenties.

In the greenhouse area (Fig. 2-B) there were also some additions. In 1924 four extra greenhouses were added, plus the cold frames, and in 1926 the buildings now known as the fig house and the vegetable house were added.

During the 1930's contacts were made with a number of nurseries and plantsmen, notably Joseph Gable of Stewartstown, Pennsylvania; Charles Dexter of Cape Cod; and Henry Hohman of Kingsville, Maryland. The emphasis was on azaleas and rhododendrons, and many choice hybrids were obtained and planted either in the cutting garden or in a nursery area of the Azalea Woods. This was the beginning of the rhododendron and azalea collections on the grand scale. In addition to the Kurume azaleas, Mr. H. F. du Pont obtained many of the Gable hybrids shortly after their introduction in the 'thirties and 'forties. This has continued with the Glenn Dale hybrid azaleas in the late 'forties and throughout the 'fifties. In the 'fifties he also procured representatives of other hybrid groups, such as the Merritt, Exbury, Beltsville, and Chugai azaleas.

The now-famous Dexter hybrid rhododendrons were obtained in quantity, as tiny seedlings during the 'thirties and grown to flowering size by Mr. H. F. du Pont. By 1945 or 1946 these plants had obtained considerable size, and at this time the Azalea Woods (Fig. 2-E), as we know it today, was laid out. The primary aim of this effort was the creation of the harmonious color scheme found throughout the area today. Seedling rhododendrons of unpleasant colors were removed and replaced with others more congenial to the location. Some were arranged in pleasing combinations with other rhododendrons and with azaleas. Many new azaleas were moved in from nursery areas, others were moved from one location to another (always with color harmony in mind), and the whole area was considerably enlarged. Some of the plants were twenty years old. One of the finest displays of very early color was achieved with the planting of twenty-four specimens of *Rhododendron praevernum* (purchased from the Dexter estate in 1944) at the extreme southeast end of the Azalea Woods, close to the steps at the bend in the road.

Other additions in 1946 were the Gable azaleas near the George and Martha Washington figures, the great banks of azalea 'Hinodegiri' and kaempferi hybrids in the area of the swings, the group of purple azaleas in front of the huge sycamore, and the many kaempferi hybrid and other azaleas along the old path to the tennis court, now the Sundial Garden (Fig. 2-M).

Today Mr. H. F. du Pont is keenly interested in primulas. This interest dates from before 1929, when the old primula quarry near the guide's parking lot was developed. At that time a number of species and hybrids were being grown, namely *Primula denticulata, P. cockburniana, P. pulverulenta,* and, in two or three years' time *P. bulleyana* and *P. beesiana.* Even meconopsis, the fabulous "Blue Poppy" of the Himalayas, almost unheard of in this section of the country, grew and bloomed in the old quarry. To be able to grow it, much less make it bloom, is a considerable accomplishment.

About 1950, work was started on Oak Hill (Fig. 2-R). Young Oaks and many of the varieties of dogwood were planted along with the Glenn Dale azaleas, philadelphus, deutzia, spirea and other June-blooming material. Once again Mr. H. F. du Pont's connection with horticultural institutions enabled him to obtain rare and fine plants for Oak Hill, this time in the form of native azaleas collected in the southern mountains by Henry Skinner, now director of the U. S. National Arboretum, but then working with the Morris Arboretum of Philadelphia. These native azaleas, which include several species and natural hybrids, have a wide range of color and bloom, many being in flower from June to August. The young plants were put in among the oaks in the early 'fifties, and have now reached a fair size, providing a good show of color each year. In the meantime, more of these native specimens have been added to the planting. In the late 'fifties a collection arrived from the Middle Atlantic Chapter of the American Rhododendron Society, and in the spring of 1963 many plants were brought in to further develop Oak Hill and extend it down to the Quarry area.

In the 'fifties, too, development of the hellebores along the Corylopsis Walk was started. Varieties of Christmas and Lenten roses, corydalis, erythronium, and other ground-cover material were planted among the corylopsis and *R. mucronulatum* (Fig. 2-J).

About 1957-58 the formal areas of the Sundial Garden were planned by Mr. H. F. du Pont (Fig. 2-M). Prior to this time, the site, enclosed on three sides by English box, had been a tennis and croquet court. The area immediately around the sundial was designed by the landscape architect, Miss Marian Coffin, whose mother had been a friend of Mr. H. F. du Pont's mother. The wonderful *Chaenomeles* 'Appleblossom' and 'Phyllis Moore,' the eight dominant features of the garden, were brought from elsewhere on the estate, as were many of the other shrubs used in this planting. *Malus* 'Henrietta Crosby' and *Prunus* 'Hally Jolivette' were acquired from Dr. Karl Sax of the Arnold Arboretum. Both of these plants, incidentally, are Dr. Sax's own originations, the prunus being named after his wife. Another of Dr. Sax's hybrids, *Malus* 'H. F. du Pont,' was received at this time and planted in the crab-apple collection in the Pinetum.

Mr. H. F. du Pont's early association with the Arnold Arboretum is responsible for many treasures among the unusual plants in the gardens. Through direct contact with such men as Prof. Sargent, E. H. Wilson, and Karl Sax, he was able to obtain rare material (much of which by today is considered part and parcel of any good garden) soon after its introduction into this country. In addition to the apples and cherries listed above, a partial list of these plants includes: *Acer griseum,* the Paper-bark Maple; *Ehretia thyrsiflora,* the Heliotrope-tree; *Forsythia* 'Beatrix Farrand,' *F.* 'Arnold Giant,' and *F. ovata* 'Spring Glory'; lilacs such as 'Isabella' and 'Crayton'; and red-flowered clones of *R. calendulaceum,* the Flame Azalea. The fact that one can find here such unusual plants of a size and age seldom encountered elsewhere in this country contributes greatly to Winterthur's distinction among American gardens.

The next area of development—the Pavilion (Fig. 2-A) and the new entrance-way and parking lot for the public—brings the history almost up to date. Started in the fall of 1960, the Pavilion was completed just in time for the opening of the Garden Tour of 1961. Its site was a swampy area that prior to 1960 had not been developed at all. As much of the natural growth as possible was saved during this operation, and this was supplemented with plantings of yew, hollies, rhododendrons, barberry and other shrubs, a collection of heathers and dwarf evergreens, and a mixed planting of daylilies and botanical tulips. Later, one of the banks near the building was planted with hostas thickly interspersed with hybrid tulips. Finally, a small rose garden was planted as a reminder of, and in a small way a replacement for, the old rose garden which had been lost a few years previously.

A walk was then laid out connecting the Pavilion with the main gardens and route to the museum. Where this walk bisected the back drive to Adams Dam Road, the roadway was raised and an underpass built. At this point a large natural planting of ferns was put in under the cool shade of oak and beech. The planting has been subsequently expanded to include nearly every species of fern that will grow in the area. In 1962 three varieties of azalea were planted in drifts along this path, between the Pavilion and the underpass. The weeds on the left side (east side) of the path were then cleared and holes dug for young rhododendrons—propagations of Winterthur's own Dexter hybrids.

In 1960 the area around and beyond the big sycamore (Fig. 2-P) was being developed in order to provide a lengthened season of bloom. Because the garden up to this time had been for the most part an April-May blooming area, and it was felt that it should be open to the public for a longer period of time, work was concentrated on providing June-July blooming material. In what was once an old cornfield were planted species lilacs, philadelphus, deutzias, late-blooming azaleas, magnolias, lilies, and other late-blooming plants. In 1962 work was continued to provide an even better selection of material there, with the inclusion of late spireas, tamarix, and late-blooming ornamental trees such as catalpas and golden-raintrees. At the southern edge of this planting, the Bristol Summerhouse was erected in 1961. This building is a replica of a summerhouse on the Colt estate in Bristol, Rhode Island (hence its name). Built on the edge of a steep slope, it commands a fine view of the valley below, with its pastures, streams, and the pond below the Quarry. Backed by a young tulip poplar, the building is flanked by ceanothus and shrub roses of a dusky rose-pink, which harmonize both in texture and color with the surroundings. The summerhouse was built in our own workshop here at Winterthur, from plans provided by an architect in Bristol.

To the north of this Sycamore area, a whole hillside has been planted with many species of viburnums from various parts of the world. Begun in 1961, the planting was extended in 1962 and 1963 as other species became available. The very latest addition to the area was the building of the "Lookout" (Fig. 2-O) during the winter of 1962-63. The Lookout is a circular structure of brick arches supporting a peaked heavy tin roof surmounted by a lead eagle with wide-spread wings. This structure sits well up on the new viburnum hill, framed from behind by an upright English oak. The imposing roof was designed by Thomas T. Waterman, a member of the Historical American Building Survey, who was architect at Winterthur from 1933 to 1950. It formerly capped a small back-building at the museum, which was torn down when the south wing was built.

In 1960-61 work was started on the Primula Quarry (Fig. 2-Q) which lies between the Sycamore area and Oak Hill. This was an actual quarry which had lain in disuse for many years. Since several springs keep its base constantly cool and wet, it was decided that the Asiatic bog primulas might thrive there, and thrive they did. Although large natural rock faces did exist in parts of the bank, other parts had begun to slough, exposing the roots of the tall trees around the rim; therefore, it was decided to supplement the existing rock with more. Once the walls were wrapped with rock, choice shrubs and plants of all kinds were introduced among them, and the primulas were spread out over the whole floor. To date, about forty species and hybrid primulas, numbering in the thousands of plants, have been grown from seed for this area, most of which have proven satisfactory. The moist run parallel to the new Pavilion drive is used for planting unknown varieties in order to see how they perform. If they are satisfactory in vigor, clarity of color, and showiness, a number of them are taken to the Quarry the following year. At the present time, the Quarry is full of colorful bloom through much of April, all of May, and most of June. During the later weeks, it is really the *pièce de résistance* of the whole garden.

Further expansion with primulas is also planned. The little stream that drains the Quarry has been recently planted with seedlings of a few choice species, and the little wild bog near the pond below the Quarry Bridge, which now contains wild orchids, marsh-marigolds, and cardinal-flower, is scheduled to be planted with the lovely pink *Primula pulverulenta* 'Bartley Strain' and the giant belled species *P. florindae*. This is being done in order to keep the 'Bartley Strain' from crossing with other species of the candelabra section. *P. florindae,* being of the belled section, will not cross with it. In addition, a portion of the Chandler Woods, located north of the Pavilion parking area, is due to be planted with the hardiest of all the candelabras, *Primula japonica.* This portion of woodland is swampy by nature and surrounded by natural stands of mountain-laurel. It is felt that this shrub, blooming at the same time as *P. japonica,* will make a wonderful combination as both plants come in all shades of pink, white, and near red.

The run parallel to the new road to the Pavilion has had drifts of *P. japonica* planted along it for a number of years. These are very effective from the road, and plans have been made to increase these plantings. In order to give more wet bank area, a series of small dams has been constructed along this stream. At the head of the stream is a wet area which will be used as a trial nursery for species with which we have had no experience. For years the azalea woods has had quantities of woodland species of primulas; these will be supplemented with new species, such as *P. elatior, P. leucophylla,* and *P. polyneura,* which are likely to do well in a woodland location.

The emphasis in 1963 has been on improving and expanding late bloom in the areas of the Sycamore, the Quarry, and on Oak Hill. A pond, dug in the spring of 1961, lies at the junction of the stream that drains the Quarry and the run coming down through the meadow. This serves as the focal point for a beautiful vista from the crest of Oak Hill as well as from the Bristol Summerhouse. It also attracts waterfowl; mallards can be seen on its surface at almost any time, and in the spring of 1963, a family of wild geese used it for a number of weeks. The stream between this pond and the Quarry has been developed with rockwork, and in addition to primulas, choice dwarf, late-flowering shrubs have been worked in among the rocks.

At the east end of Oak Hill near the Quarry Bridge, several groups of native azaleas have been added, including a large planting of the Plumleaf Azalea *(R. prunifolium)*, a species from Georgia that bears bright orange-red flowers in July and August. Here also has been added a group of shrubs and trees valuable for their ornamental fruit. These include snowberry, tea viburnum, beautyberry, trifoliate orange, and the Oriental persimmon. They make an impressive display, with their variously-sized fruits of yellow, orange, white, and bright lilac. The slope below these is covered with masses of lilac colchicum.

These garden annals would certainly not be complete without a mention of the developments planned for the Oak Hill area. A new grass walk has been made along the existing ridge halfway down Oak Hill, extending from the Quarry Bridge to the present planting of lilacs, deutzias, spireas, and philadelphus. Above this walk, the original collection of native azaleas will be expanded, using propagations from these old plants which are now ready in the nursery. Below the walk the hillside will be covered with, first, Mouse-ear Hawkweed *(Hieracium flagellare)*, which will be brought in from another part of the garden. This is a dwarf wild plant with showy yellow daisy-like blooms. Next will be a drift of the dusky rose-pink *Silene armeria,* one of the campions of the pink family, and following will be groups of two species of indigo, the dwarf white *Indigofera incarnata alba* and the slightly taller pink *I. kirilowi.* Further down the hill will be a large group of a rose-pink Steeple-bush, *Spirea billiardi.* At this point along the path will be several plants of *Leptodermis oblonga,* with tubular mauve flowers. These will be planted at the edge of the existing planting of pink and white spirea and deutzia, mauve and pink lilacs, and white philadelphus. Further in, along the woodland edge, will be grouped the Japanese azalea 'Beni-kirishima,' a late double red.

The walk will continue through the large shrubs here and finally turn upwards to meet the existing walk across the top of Oak Hill. These new additions will not only enliven the color in the area; they will help to present the visitor with an unbroken series of June-blooming plants from the time he leaves the Sundial Garden to the time he leaves Oak Hill. Actually, June is one of the loveliest months at Winterthur. The trunks of the huge oaks and tulip poplars, and the many shades of green among the trees and shrubs, present a quiet, restful contrast to the brilliance of April and May.

A beautiful garden is a work of art, but, unlike a painting or a book, a garden grows. Component parts alter; results change; new vistas open, bringing new ideas and, in time, new effects. This organic growth makes gardening one of the most challenging and one of the most rewarding of the arts. It is hoped that these few pages may give the reader some idea of this organic growth, as well as an idea of Mr. H. F. du Pont's vast amount of time, knowledge, and work, not to speak of plant material involved, so that he may further enjoy Winterthur in all its facets, knowing that it is here for posterity.

The Winterthur Program
in Early American Culture:

An Experiment in a Joint-Institutional, Inter-disciplinary Curriculum

By WAYNE CRAVEN

On October 30, 1951, Mr. Henry Francis du Pont made his collection of early American furniture and decorative arts available to the public. But even as Winterthur Museum came into being, it was envisioned as something more than a sanctuary for artifacts of Americana, for it was to assume the role of teacher as well as conservator. At the opening ceremonies, John Alanson Perkins, president of the University of Delaware spoke of a collaboration of the Museum and the University to this end: "As a schoolmaster, I am impelled to point out that Winterthur . . . is an educational institution. It promises to fulfill its educational function more completely than most museums do. . . . The same circumstances which have attracted brilliant young scientific talent to our community should henceforth attract equally promising students of the arts and the humanities. The whole nation will benefit by having available more capable and better educated students of Americana for the staffs of libraries, museums, and universities."

Earlier in 1951, with the encouragement of Mr. du Pont, President Perkins and Mr. Charles F. Montgomery, then associate curator of the Museum and later director, met to discuss the idea of a graduate program to train students in the fields of American civilization as well as connoisseurship and conservation of the decorative arts and fine arts of this country. President Perkins immediately invited several members of his administrative staff and the faculty from the departments of history, English, and art to the meeting to comment on the organization of the Program and to make suggestions about the curriculum. From the beginning then, instruction was to come from several disciplines within the humanities; added to

Fig. 1 John A. Perkins, Henry F. du Pont, and Charles F. Montgomery, *photographed in 1954, on the occasion of the graduation exercises of the first fellows of the Winterthur Program in Early American Culture.*

Fig. 2 Fellows of the class of 1965 with Ernest J. Moyne *(at blackboard): Nancy E. Richards, Cary Carson, Barbara Louise Gilbert, Cynthia Anne Pease, John H. Hill, David B. Warren, James R. Mitchell.*

this academic curriculum were courses in the decorative arts to be taught by specialists on the staff of the Museum. The goal was to be the study of American civilization in the seventeenth, eighteenth, and nineteenth centuries through an analysis of the historic events, the literature and philosophy, and the visual arts: architecture, painting, sculpture, and the decorative and utilitarian arts. The potentials of the project grew large in the minds of those present, and very soon definite steps were taken to turn potentiality into reality.

The initial discussions about the Museum-University sponsored program were carried on in the first half of 1951. On July 30th of that year the Committee on Graduate Studies at the University approved the Program and the Board of Trustees did the same on December 8, 1951. At that time the name used was "The Program in American Decorative Arts." A memorandum to the Board of Directors of the Winterthur Corporation from Mr. Lammot du Pont Copeland, chairman of the Finance Committee, reads: "July 18, 1951. Mr. Charles Montgomery advised the Committee that he had had discussions with the president and other members of the staff of the University of Delaware as to the possibilities of the University granting Master degrees in the field of American Decorative Arts to qualified students who have spent two years at the Henry Francis du Pont Winterthur Museum (and) . . . the University."

A grant from the Rockefeller Foundation signally aided the launching of the Program. The University needed funds to provide released time for those members of the faculty who were working in the Program in order that specialized seminars could be taught, and research encouraged. The teaching staff of certain departments had to be increased, and money was needed to improve the holdings of the University library in the fields of the decorative arts, architecture, and American civilization. President Perkins, with the assistance of Professor Ernest J. Moyne, Professor Frank H. Sommer, and Dean Carl J. Rees, prepared a prospectus of the project which was submitted to the Rockefeller Foundation. In anticipation of queries which were sure to be posed, the Program's goals had to be clarified. Why should the project be undertaken at all and what would the graduates do after they had received their degrees? Mr. Montgomery replied to both questions by pointing out that nowhere could one acquire formal university preparation for curatorial work in the American wing of art museums, in historical societies, or in restorations of historic houses, and that the Program would offer a new approach for the study of American culture. As a study of American civilization, the Winterthur Program was unique in that it placed major emphasis on the fine arts, whereas other American Studies curricula stressed either literature or social history.

Mr. Edward F. D'Arms of the Rockefeller Foundation visited Winterthur and Newark to discuss the project. He was especially attracted by the inter-disciplinary, even joint-institutional, curriculum and by the fact that such an educational program could spread far and wide to reach great numbers of people, giving Americans a better understanding of their heritage. In 1952, the Rockefeller Foundation granted $75,000.00 to the University of Delaware for the Winterthur Program, to be spent over the next three years. Later, the Avalon Foundation made an additional grant of $10,000.00 to carry on the work.

Thus assured of inaugural funds, the Program began to take form, but the problems were immense. Nowhere was there an established course of a comparable nature which could serve as a model. Although the Winterthur Program has now become a pilot for others, it was then a pioneer effort. A curriculum had to be devised, and qualified students had to be informed of the new and unknown Program. A two-year course of study was organized, with instruction divided between seminars at the University and laboratory work at the Museum.[1]

Brochures describing the Program were drawn up and mailed to institutions and to individuals who would have contact with interested and qualified persons, especially seniors graduating from college. Many personal letters were written by the faculty and the Museum staff to colleagues at other universities, museums, and historical societies in an effort to reach a greater number of potential students. To attract a high calibre of student, who could not personally finance the two years of graduate training, Mr. Montgomery obtained five $2,000.00 fellowships, renewable for the student's second year of study, from a group of benefactors who were interested in the Museum. In this he was greatly assisted by Mr. Walter J. Laird, then treasurer of the Winterthur Corporation, and Mr. M. Alfred E. Bissel who succeeded Mr. Laird as treasurer. The following entry is found in the Minutes of the Annual Meeting of Directors of the Winterthur Corporation, under date of January 8, 1952: "Mr. Montgomery announced that two Fellowships had been pledged, one by Mr. C. K. Davis, and one by *Antiques Magazine*. Mrs. Francis B. Crowninshield then stated that she would give a Fellowship, which was accepted with the gratitude of the Board. " The helpful and loyal friends who have assisted the young enterprise throughout the dozen years of its existence through the gift of fellowships are listed at the end of this article.

Applications to the Program were received and the first class of Winterthur students, recipients of fellowships, was selected. After the formation of the Winterthur Committee (members of the University faculty and administration and of the Museum staff directly connected with the Winterthur Program), the selection of the fellows was achieved in the following manner. Applications were returned to the coordinator of the Winterthur Program, and the Committee chose ten or twelve on the basis of academic achievement, previous experience in work in some aspect of American civilization, and an expression of sincere and enthusiastic interest in the Program. A final committee of selection, composed of several members of the Board of Directors of the Winterthur Museum and representatives from

---

[1] The original thirty-hour curriculum, now considerably augmented, consisted of the following courses:

FIRST YEAR	SECOND YEAR
First Semester:	*First Semester:*
Sources of American Art	Studies in Colonial Literature
17th and 18th Century England	American Colonial Life
American Decorative Arts	Thesis
Second Semester:	*Second Semester:*
The American Tradition	Life in the Early Republic
English Composition	English Composition
American Decorative Arts	Thesis

Currently the English Composition courses have been dropped, and more specialized art history courses have been added.

the University of Delaware administration and faculty, invited the most qualified candidates to visit Winterthur and Newark for a personal interview and to examine the facilities of the two institutions. Within a few days, five of the applicants were notified that they had been awarded fellowships. The above procedure is in general still followed except that now others may be invited to enroll in the Program at their own expense.

And so, with a commitment to a group of Master's candidates due to arrive in the fall of 1952 and a concept of what the Program was to become, the Winterthur Program was launched.

The Winterthur Committee first met as a body on a Sunday afternoon in September of 1952 in the office of Dr. Carl J. Rees, dean of the Graduate School of the University of Delaware. Present from the faculty and administration of the University were, in addition to Dr. Rees, Dr. Frank Squire, dean of the School of Arts and Science; Professors John A. Munroe, H. Clay Reed and Walter L. Woodfill (Department of History); Frank H. Sommer (Department of Sociology and Anthropology); Harriet Baily (Department of Art); Ernest J. Moyne (Department of English); and Mr. William D. Lewis, librarian. Mr. Montgomery, who, with his wife, Florence M. Montgomery, taught the first decorative arts courses at Winterthur, represented the Museum. Dr. Sommer was elected coordinator, a post he held for three years, while Dr. Moyne—who was to succeed him as coordinator from 1955 to 1962—agreed to act as secretary. The group met formally every two weeks.

In selecting the name, "The Winterthur Program in Early American Culture," the Committee insured an inter-disciplinary approach to the study of American civilization, and created a curriculum which utilized the artifact as well as the document in the interpretation of that civilization. "Art cannot be understood in terms of 'pure form.' Architecture, town planning, and the design of utilitarian objects such as furniture and pottery are man's solution to the problem of daily living. The objects become fully intelligible only when studied in relation to those problems. Representational painting and sculpture can be fully understood only if one considers their iconography and symbolism as well as their forms. Since the problems created and solved, and the meaning of iconography and symbolism are socially and culturally determined, art must be studied within the framework of culture and society." [2] Hence, the disciplines of sociology, economics, history, philosophy, theology, literature as well as art history and anthropology were brought to bear on the artifact.

Also accompanying the growth of the Winterthur Program for graduate students was the formation of an American Studies curriculum for undergraduates at the University. Later, the Hagley Program, an enterprise similar to the Winterthur Program, but stressing the history of industry, business, and technology, was established at the University and Hagley Museum near Wilmington to make this scholarly community an even more complete center for the study and interpretation of the many phases of American civilization.

Between the combined resources of the University and the Museum, the Program was fortunate in finding many well-qualified scholars and connoisseurs among its own ranks. But such a specialized project could hardly

---

[2] From the initial prospectus presented to the Rockefeller Foundation.

expect to find a ready-made faculty immediately on the scene. Therefore, a certain amount of the Rockefeller Foundation grant was allotted to an annual series of visits and lectures by distinguished men and women in fields related to the Winterthur Program. Eminent scholars and specialists were invited to Delaware, one about every two weeks from October to May. These visiting scholars brought the depth of their learning in specialized areas into seminar meetings with students and staff; they presented public lectures, and met informally with interested persons. The visiting scholar program familiarized people in museums, universities, and historical societies across the country with the newly established Winterthur Program, with the result that many of the fellows from various areas throughout the United States applied to the Program at the suggestion of visiting Winterthur lecturers.

With the passing of the years the nature and purpose of the Winterthur Lecture Series has changed significantly, largely as the result of changes which have occurred in the teaching staff of the Program. At the University of Delaware, Dr. G. Bruce Dearing, who has been dean of the School of Arts and Science since 1957, has taken a vigorous interest in the Program, introducing measures to encourage the faculty's activity in research in and teaching of American civilization. Dr. Alan Gowans was appointed chairman of the Department of Art (now Department of Art and Art History). Realizing the need for a larger instructional staff to work in the Program, Mr. Henry Francis du Pont initially provided three professorial chairs at the University. In the fall of 1960, Dr. George Frick (History), Dr. Calhoun Winton (English), who became coordinator of the Program in 1962, and the writer (Department of Art and Art History) joined the University faculty as Henry Francis du Pont Assistant Professors, and began teaching in the Program. Mr. Edmond du Pont currently underwrites these three chairs. In the Department of History, Dr. Robert A. Smith replaced Dr. Walter Woodfill, after the latter left to teach at the University of California at Davis in 1961.

Changes have also occurred in the staff of the Museum involved in the Winterthur Program. In 1958, Dr. Albert S. Roe, an art historian, joined the Museum staff to teach some of the Winterthur classes held there, in addition to his other responsibilities with the painting and print collections.[3] Dr. Sommer, who had left the University and the Program in 1955, returned to the latter as a member of the Museum personnel in 1958. The addition of an art historian and an anthropologist thus enriched the teaching staff at the Museum. They, along with Mr. and Mrs. Montgomery provided instruction in the American decorative arts and their origins, concentrating mainly on interior design, furniture, silver, glass, textiles, ceramics, and other crafts. Mr. Montgomery, who had been appointed director of the Museum in 1954, resigned that office in 1962 to devote his efforts to research and teaching. At times other members of the Museum staff have helped to direct the research and writing of the fellows' theses. In 1955, Dr. E. McClung Fleming came to the Museum as head of its educational program. He has served as liaison between the Museum and the University, and for several years has acted as secretary of the Winterthur Committee.

---

[3] Dr. Roe left the Museum to become chairman of the Department of Art History at Cornell University in 1961.

As the faculty increased in size and degree of specialization, and as the Winterthur Program became better known across the country and abroad, the role of the Winterthur lecturers gradually changed. At first intended to supplement the teaching staff by spending collectively many weeks on campus and at the Museum, with numerous lectures, seminars, and informal discussions, the visiting specialists currently stay only about two days each, and the number per year has been reduced. They now give only one public lecture, participate in one or another of the Winterthur seminar classes, tour the Museum, and meet informally with the students and staff. Their hosts are usually members of the faculty or Museum staff, the president of the University or the director of the Museum.

The aim and quality of the Program have become known not only through word being carried abroad by these visiting scholars and specialists, but also by publications of members of the Winterthur Committee or former fellows. Three Winterthur theses have been published: John A. H. Sweeney's *Grandeur on the Appoquinimink* (University of Delaware Press, 1959), Jean McClure Mudge's *Chinese Export Porcelain for American Trade, 1785-1835* (University of Delaware Press, 1962), and Jesse Poesch's *Titian Ramsay Peale* (The American Philosophical Society, 1961). Further research by former Winterthur fellows has led to such publications as: *The Adams Papers* (The Belknap Press), of which Wendell Garrett is associate editor, and *Apthorp House, 1760-1960* (Adams House, Harvard University, 1960), by the same author, and John Sweeney's *Winterthur Illustrated* (The Henry Francis du Pont Winterthur Museum, Inc., 1963), (cloth edition, *The Treasure House of Early American Rooms: A Winterthur Book,* Viking Press, 1963). Lorraine Pierce's text for the guidebook, *The White House* (White House Historical Association, 1962), may also be cited. Those teaching in the Winterthur Program have also brought out several books: Dr. John A. Munroe has written *Federalist Delaware, 1775-1815* (Rutgers University Press, 1954), and Professor Alan Gowans has published *Looking at Architecture in Canada* (Oxford University Press, 1958) and *Images of American Living* (Lippincott, 1963). Dr. Frick has written a study of the American naturalist artist, *Mark Catesby* (University of Illinois Press, 1961), and Dr. Winton's book, *Captain Steele, the Early Career of Richard Steele,* has gone to press; *American Painting, 1857-69,* was prepared by the writer of the present article as the catalogue of a similarly entitled exhibition of paintings shown at the Delaware Art Center and jointly sponsored with the University. Mr. Charles Montgomery has published his *Some Remarks on the Science and Principles of Connoisseurship* (The Walpole Society, 1961). In addition, numerous articles on diverse aspects of American civilization and its arts have appeared in both scholarly and popular periodicals.

A graduate program seldom advances at a pace which exceeds the growth of its library. In the early years of the Program, a portion of the Rockefeller grant was devoted to the purchase, for the University Library, of books on the arts, history, and literature of America. The generosity of Mrs. Esther Schwartz has assisted greatly in the formation of a specialized library in the American decorative arts at the University of Delaware, and over the years the Winterthur libraries have also added large numbers of rare, useful, and beautiful volumes.

The libraries of the Museum, which are continually being enlarged in the various areas of American civilization, and the Museum's collections of the decorative arts are two of the greatest assets which the Program has to offer to the student. The Program brings five to eight graduate students each year to the University and the Museum for two years of study; a number of these students will be recipients of fellowships, which have now been increased to $2,500.00 a year. Study begins several weeks before regular classes commence at the University, when the new students (referred to as the First Year Fellows) complete a course at the Museum which is designed to familiarize them immediately with the collections. Through classroom lectures and study conducted in the period rooms, the students are introduced to the different facets of the arts in America. This also prepares them to act as guides for visitors to the Museum a few hours each week during most of their two years in the Program; guiding gives the fellow experience in interpreting and explaining the collections to visitors, and also assures a regular review of all aspects of the collections.

In September, the First Year Fellows begin taking courses, usually conducted as seminars, at the University and the Museum. The student may be asked to prepare one or several documented research papers on some aspect of American civilization; these may or may not be presented orally in class. This practice not only gives the student experience in research but also in written and oral presentation. The relatively small number of students in each class permits free discussion of any comments or questions pertinent to the subject at hand. Primary research and analysis of the objects available in the collections of the Museum are encouraged in every aspect of the Program. Mastery of fundamental factual information, research, methodology, and training in connoisseurship are the goals of these classes. This inter-disciplinary curriculum is intended to give the student an integrated view of the diverse aspects of American civilization.

Requirements for the Master of Arts in Early American Culture are greater than those for most Master of Arts degrees. Forty-two hours of course credits in social history, literature, history of art (with special emphasis on the decorative arts), and connoisseurship are necessary as well as a thesis involving primary research. The student selects his thesis subject during the spring semester of the first year, and an adviser is appointed by the Committee. The student devotes the following summer to research on the subject and to the writing of the first draft. Thesis research is done wherever the source material is to be found—anywhere from New England to New Mexico. Returning in the fall, the student is a Second Year Fellow and continues with the preparation of his thesis. In the past, thesis subjects have ranged from "Joseph Richardson, Quaker Silversmith" to "Baltimore's Washington Monument," to "Washington Irving's Interest in Art and His Influence upon American Painting" and to "The Sullivan Dorr House in Providence, Rhode Island." Altogether, then, two full years of academic work, one complete summer and part of another, plus a thesis are required. A demanding program, indeed, but one which is intended to produce a well-trained person prepared to assume immediate responsibility in art museums or historical societies, to continue graduate work for the Doctor of Philosophy degree, or to assume any one of the many other professional duties listed at the end of this article.

CLASS	COLLEGE - DEGREE	PRESENT POSITION
1954		
Fales, Mrs. Dean A. (Martha Lou Gandy)	B.A. Wilson	Honorary Curator of Silver Essex Institute
Munier, Mrs. Robert C.	B.A. Scripps	Director Wenham Historical Assoc. and Museum, Inc.
Schwartz, Marvin D.	B.S. City College of New York	Curator, Decorative Arts Brooklyn Museum
Sweeney, John A. H.	B.A. Yale	Curator, Winterthur Museum
Hunter, Dard, Jr. (special student)		Curator, Adena State Memorial
1955		
Clark, Raymond B., Jr.	B.A. Washington M.A. Univ. of Penna.	Northern Virginia Branch University of Virginia
Hummel, Charles F.	B.A. City College of New York	Associate Curator, Winterthur Museum
Lindsay, G. Carroll	B.A. Franklin & Marshall	Curator, Smithsonian Museum Service
Naeve, Milo M.	B.F.A. University of Colorado	Registrar, Winterthur Museum
1956		
Poesch, Jessie J.	B.A. Antioch	Assistant Professor of Art Newcomb College Tulane University
Prown, Jules	B.A. Lafayette Ph.D. Harvard	Instructor, History of Art Yale University
Prown, Mrs. Jules (Shirley A. Martin)	B.A. Wilson	Housewife
Roth, Rodris C.	B.A. Univ. of Minn.	Associate Curator, Division of Cultural History Smithsonian Institution
Stillman, S. Damie	B.S. Northwestern U. Ph.D. Columbia Univ.	Assistant Professor of Art History, Michigan State U.
1957		
Butler, Joseph T.	B.S. Md. State Teachers M.A. Ohio University	Curator, Sleepy Hollow Restorations
Creer, Doris	B.A. Pomona	Delaware Art Center Education Assistant
Dunbar, Mrs. Maxwell J. (Nancy Wosstroff)	B.S. Skidmore	Curator of Exhibits Redpath Museum McGill University
Garrett, Wendell	B.A. U.C.L.A.	Associate Editor, The Adams Papers Mass. Historical Society
Mudge, Mrs. Lewis S. (Jean McClure)	B.A. Stamford Univ.	Housewife

1958

Ahlborn, Richard E.	B.F.A. Colorado	Curator, Joslyn Art Museum Omaha, Nebraska
Huber, Mrs. Charles (Mary Means)	B.A. Wheaton	Housewife
Nonemaker, James	B.A. Rutgers	Director, Harris County Heritage Society
Pearce, Mrs. John (Lorraine Waxman)	B.S. City College of New York	Curator of White House to 7/1/62 — Housewife
Rubenstein, Lewis C.	B.A. Cornell	Curator of History, John Jay House Katonah, New York

1959

Hanson, Frederick	B.F.A. Syracuse Univ.	Curator of Decorative Arts National Park Service
Knapp, Mrs. Edwin H. (Ruth Matzkin)	B.A. Penna. Univ.	Housewife
Pearce, John N.	B.A. Yale	Assistant Curator of Cultural History Smithsonian Institution
Raley, Robert	B.Arch. Notre Dame Beaux Arts M.A.Arch. Penna. Univ.	Architect
Schmidt, Frank J.	B.A. Aquinas College Marquette Univ.	Head of the Historic Sites and Properties of the Pennsylvania Historical and Museum Commission

1960

Cox, Ruth Y.	B.A. William & Mary	Curatorial Assistant, Textiles, Colonial Williamsburg
Hawley, Henry H.	B.A. Stanford M.A. Harvard	Assistant Curator of Decorative Arts Cleveland Museum of Art
Hendrick, Robert E. P.	B.A. Yale	Curatorial Assistant Colonial Williamsburg
Milley, John C.	B.A. Boston Univ.	Museum Curator Independence National Historical Park Philadelphia, Pennsylvania
Smith, Stuart B.	B.A. Carroll College	United States Navy

1961

Brown, Robert F.	A.B. Brown University	Fulbright Scholar Birkbeck College University of London
Cayford, Jane L.	A.B. Pembroke College	Director—as of 7/10/63 New Hampshire Historical Society
Fairbanks, Jonathan L.	B.F.A. Univ. Utah M.F.A. Univ. Penna.	Assistant Curator Winterthur Museum
Gilborn, Craig A.	B.A. Michigan State	Program Administrator Virginia Museum of Fine Arts Richmond, Virginia
Hyder, Darrell D.	A.B. Stanford Univ.	United States Army

1962

Castrodale, Anne	A.B. Penn State	Assistant Curator, Growth of the United States Department of Civil History Smithsonian Institution
Davis, John D.	B.A. Oberlin	United States Army
Greenlaw, Barry A.	A.B. Bates College	Director, Old Gaol Museum York, Maine
Miller, J. Jefferson, II	A.B. John Hopkins L.L.D. U. of Md.	Assistant Curator Div. of Ceramics and Glass Smithsonian Institution
Rippe, Peter M.	A.B. Univ. of Puget Sound	Head of Research Confederate Museum Richmond, Virginia

1963

Doud, Richard K.	B.F.A. Colorado U.	Field Researcher, Archives of American Art, Detroit, Mich.
Goyne, Nancy	B.S. U. of Del.	Curatorial Assistant, Winterthur Museum
Hoberg, Perry F.	B.F.A.-B.S. Ed. Temple Univ.	Instructor of History P.S. du Pont High School
Johnson, Marilynn A.	B.A. Duke Univ.	Cataloguer, Winterthur Museum
Leibundguth, Arthur W.	B.A. Luther Chicago Univ.	Director, Antiquarian and Landmarks Society of Connecticut, Inc.
Quimby, Ian M. G.	B.A. U. of Del.	Merrimack Textile Museum, Curator North Andover, Massachusetts
Webster, Richard J.	B.A. Lafayette	Instructor of Social Studies Temple Univ. Community College

DONORS OF WINTERTHUR FELLOWSHIPS

Antiques Magazine
Mr. and Mrs. Alfred E. Bissell
Mrs. Lammot du Pont Copeland
Mr. Lammot du Pont Copeland
The Copeland Andelot Foundation
The Crestlea Foundation
Mrs. Francis B. Crowninshield (permanently endowed Fellowship)
Mr. Charles K. Davis
Mr. Edmond du Pont
Mr. Henry Belin du Pont
Mr. Pierre S. du Pont
Mrs. Jackson A. Dykman
The Eleutherian Mills-Hagley Foundation
Mr. and Mrs. Alfred C. Harrison
The Harrison Charitable Trust
Mrs. A. Duer Irving, in memory of Commander A. Duer Irving, USNRF
Mr. and Mrs. George de Forest Lord
Norumbega Fund (George de Forest Lord)
Mrs. Beverley R. Robinson, in memory of Beverley R. Robinson
Dr. Robert O. Y. Warren
The Welfare Foundation, Incorporated
Wilmington Trust Company

Joseph Downs, Curator,
Winterthur Museum, 1949-1954

THE WINTERTHUR LIBRARIES:
AN INTRODUCTORY NOTE

The collections of papers, drawings, photographs, books, and periodicals which today constitute the Winterthur libraries began to grow in 1839 as the private library of the creators of the estate. During the lifetime of Colonel Henry Algernon du Pont, substantial additions were made in the realms of genealogy, horticulture, and materials dealing with the history of the war between the States. It was, however, his son, Mr. Henry Francis du Pont, who was responsible for the creation of the present collection of Americana and for shifting the emphasis of the libraries to the fields of American art and its European background. Under the leadership of the late Mr. Downs and of Mr. Montgomery the latter emphasis was continued and greatly developed.

Since 1952, Miss Helen Belknap has catalogued the books and periodicals and pushed on into the realm of social history, while continuing to develop the art collections. Today, as a result of reorganization instituted in 1963 by the present director, the head of the Library Division supervises four distinct collections and an autonomous library within the Library Division. These are the Printed Book and Periodical Collection, the Downs Manuscript and Microfilm Collection, the Slide and Photographic Collection, a special collection devoted exclusively to photographs of soundly documented works of American decorative art, and the Waldron Phoenix Belknap, Jr., Research Collection of American Painting. The last of these was made available to the museum by the generous gift of Mrs. Waldron Phoenix Belknap, Sr., in 1956 as a memorial to her son's distinguished work in the field of the study of early American painting and its English sources.

We are as yet a young institution. A great deal of building lies ahead of us. But our research materials already are rich.

To give the reader an idea of the progress which has been made and the materials which are already available to the serious scholar, the present librarian of the Downs Collection has been asked by the editors of the Winterthur Portfolio *to write the following excellent history of the creation of the assemblage of manuscripts and microfilm now in her charge.*

FRANK H. SOMMER
Head of the Library Division

The Joseph Downs Manuscript and Microfilm Library

By ELIZABETH A. INGERMAN

> *. . . collections, scholars, publications—these are the three essential elements of the learned process, and the second two are dependant upon the first. To make a collection that stores up something of importance to society and then place it at society's disposal is to store up civilization for posterity's use.*

These words from the final chapter of Wilmarth S. Lewis's autobiographical *Collector's Progress* [1] were written about Mr. Lewis's own collection of Walpoliana rather than about Winterthur, but, as a member of the Board of Directors of the Winterthur Corporation, he could hardly have spoken more cogently had he been asked to elucidate the motivation behind the forming of the Winterthur collections, the opening of Winterthur as a museum, and its development as a center of research for the study of the American arts.

When Winterthur's doors were opened in October, 1951, the general public at last had an opportunity to see the treasures that had until that time been shown only to friends of Henry Francis du Pont and to the small groups that were permitted to visit Winterthur once each month. But even before making his collections available to posterity, Mr. du Pont realized the necessity of describing and interpreting them. One of the outstanding authorities on the American decorative arts, and a person well known to Mr. du Pont, was Joseph Downs, curator of the American Wing of the Metropolitan Museum of New York. In 1949, Mr. Downs, and an associate, Mr. Charles Montgomery, accepted the task of cataloguing and publishing the Winterthur collections, Downs to have the title of curator.

For almost as many years as Mr. du Pont had been assembling the

---

[1] (New York, 1951), p. 253.

Winterthur collections, Joseph Downs had been studying the American decorative arts. His career was marked by the good fortune which had always found him in an advantageous position at a time and place when exciting things were happening. Even the barest outline of his professional life is revealing. Graduating from the Boston Museum School in 1921, he won a coveted travel scholarship which enabled him to study in Europe. Thereafter he was on the staff of the Boston Museum of Fine Arts for a time, then moved to New York where he spent two years designing furniture. From 1925 until 1932, Downs was assistant curator, then curator, of Decorative Arts at the Pennsylvania Museum of Art (now the Philadelphia Museum of Art). In 1932 he went to the Metropolitan Museum of New York, where he remained until 1949.[2]

Arriving at the Pennsylvania Museum in his thirtieth year, only a few months before the noted architectural historian and preservationist, Fiske Kimball, was appointed director, Downs came into contact with an extremely wide range of objects—from Italian medals, Gothic tapestries, and English and American Chippendale furniture to Pennsylvania German arts and crafts. His role in furnishing and describing the Fairmount Park houses under the care of the Museum was an important factor in the development of his career, providing him with an intimate knowledge of the architectural and furniture-making achievements of Philadelphia. During Mr. Down's first year in Philadelphia his earliest known professional publication, on the subject of the Tower Hill room, appeared in the October, 1925, issue of *The Pennsylvania Museum Bulletin*.[3]

Two months later he published a catalogue of a loan exhibition of Windsor chairs and Pennsylvania German painted chests.[4] During his eight years with the Pennsylvania Museum, Downs was the author of 48 publications, over half of which dealt with American subjects. Some were very brief, but all were written in his characteristically descriptive, scholarly style.

In announcing the appointment of Joseph Downs as associate curator of Decorative Arts, the *Metropolitan Museum Bulletin* for April 1932 exclaimed: "With two experts in the American decorative arts on the department staff of such competence as Mr. Downs and Miss [Ruth] Ralston, the Museum may well be congratulated."[5] Two years later the Department of Decorative Arts was reorganized to allow the American Wing, which had opened ten years earlier, to become a separate department with Mr. Downs as curator.

The guiding light and guardian angel of the American Wing from the time of its opening in 1924 until his death in 1942 was R. T. Haines Halsey, a member of the Metropolitan's Board of Trustees and chairman of the Committee for the American Wing. Mr. Halsey took a personal interest in Joseph Downs, and in 1935 sponsored the curator's membership in the Walpole Society, of which he himself was a charter member. The qualifica-

[2] HENRY FRANCIS DU PONT, "Joseph Downs. An Appreciation and a Bibliography of his Publications," *Walpole Society Note Book* (1954), pp. 36-37.

[3] "The Tower Hill Room," Pennsylvania Museum Bulletin, XXI (October, 1925), 4-11.

[4] Pennsylvania Museum, *Catalogue of a Loan Exhibition: Windsor Chairs from the Collection of J. Stodgell Stokes and Pennsylvania German Painted Chests from the Collection of Clarence Wilson Brazer* (Philadelphia, 1925).

[5] XXVII (April, 1932), 113.

tions for membership as set forth in the same year that Downs was accepted show the high ideals of the group:

> *The Walpole Society defines the qualifications for membership as distinction in the collecting of early American objects of decorative and other arts, attainment through study or experience in the knowledge of these arts; and the social qualifications essential to the well-being of a group of like-minded persons.*[6]

The years prior to Halsey's death were, perhaps, Down's most productive years with the Metropolitan. During that time the American Wing sponsored a number of important exhibitions for which special catalogues were published: *A Loan Exhibition of New York State Furniture* (1934), *Benjamin Franklin and His Circle* (1936), *American Pewterers and Their Marks* (show 1939, publication 1940), *The China Trade and Its Influences* (1941). Only one exhibition catalogue—*The Greek Revival in the United States* (1943) was published after Halsey's death. Mr. Halsey was a lender to three of the shows and wrote an introduction for the catalogue of *Benjamin Franklin and His Circle*. Significantly, a fellow Walpolian, Henry Francis du Pont, was also a lender to three of the exhibitions.

When Joseph Downs resigned to become curator of Winterthur the *Metropolitan Museum Bulletin* was fully appreciative of his contributions:

> *... During his fifteen years in that office the Museum's collections of American decorative arts have grown steadily in scope and importance . . At every point the quality of the exhibits in the American Wing has been heightened and their interest broadened through Mr. Downs's curatorship. In certain categories he has been responsible for the acquisition of virtually our entire collection. At his instigation and under his supervision a number of notable special exhibitions have been staged that have enabled the public and students to evaluate our permanent collections in a larger context ... Mr. du Pont's collection, the largest and finest of its kind, is destined to become a foundation of the very first importance for the study of early American arts. Mr. Downs carries with him the best wishes of the Trustees and Staff for his new and important assignment as well as the gratitude of the Metropolitan that he will be able to continue as an advisory member of the Staff.*[7]

Mr. Downs was drawn to Winterthur because he wanted more time to write than administrative duties in public museums had allowed. At this time he was a polished writer with over 150 publications to his credit. With his arrival at Winterthur in January, 1949, Downs quickly began collecting material for a multi-volume study of American furniture in the Winterthur Collections. He put researchers to work in the Boston area, in Philadelphia, and in New York, digging out information on cabinetmakers and furniture. In celebration of the opening of the Museum in 1951 he collaborated with Alice Winchester to produce a special issue of *Antiques.*[8] During the following year his monumental *American Furniture, Queen Anne and Chippendale Periods* [9] was published—his first, and last, full-length book. In

---

[6] *The Walpole Society Note Book* (1935), p. 9.

[7] *Metropolitan Museum Bulletin,* VII (February, 1941), 151.

[8] *Antiques, LX* (November, 1951), 402-452.

[9] JOSEPH DOWNS, *American Furniture, Queen Anne and Chippendale Periods* (New York: The Macmillan Company, 1952).

1954 Joseph Downs died, leaving notes and photographs for three unfinished volumes on American furniture—symbols of the unfulfilled ambitions of a scholar who had just begun to reach the peak of his abilities and whose loss was acutely felt at Winterthur. In the "Minutes" of the Board of Directors of the Winterthur Corporation for September 1954, the following short memorial is recorded:

> *Joseph Downs, as Curator of the Henry Francis du Pont Winterthur Museum, won a place of esteem in this community and in the hearts of each member of the Board of Directors of the Winterthur Corporation.*
>
> *He was an outstanding authority on American decorative art and was recognized as prominent in the field of fine arts. His general acclaim as a master in this field was due in part to his authoritative writings, but principally it stemmed from his command of detail and his untiring devotion and love for his chosen profession . . .*
>
> *His accomplishments and his positions of responsibility are known to all. He came to The Henry Francis du Pont Winterthur Museum after almost twenty years as Curator of the American Wing of the Metropolitan Museum of Art.*
>
> *NOW THEREFORE BE IT RESOLVED, that his knowledge and familiarity with the problems which confronted this Board in the operation of the Museum were an inspiration to those of us less schooled in the arts than he. His consultation and advice were followed not alone because of the hallmark of authority which they bore, but as well for the spirit in which they were offered. Like so many of those who have scaled the heights, Joseph Downs seemed to gain by the giving. He was modest and ever helpful. In his death we have lost invaluable counsel. Although his position as Curator may be filled, in the memory of each of us he will ever retain his place as a tried and true friend.*[10]

To those unfamiliar with the history of the Joseph Downs Manuscript and Microfilm Collection it may seem strange that a collection of manuscripts was chosen as a means of perpetuating the memory of a man who was a connoisseur of American furniture rather than a collector of manuscripts. The story of the establishment of the memorial is told in a series of letters which were submitted to the Board of Directors under the title "Proposal for the Establishment of the Joseph Downs Manuscript Collection at Winterthur."[11] The initial letter was sent by John A. H. Sweeney, then a recently graduated member of the first class of the Winterthur Program, who has since become the first person to follow Downs in the position of curator of the Museum, to Charles F. Montgomery, who had recently been appointed director:

September 23, 1954

Dear Mr. Montgomery:

> *It has occurred to me in working with inventories these past few weeks how vital this manuscript material is to the interpretation of the decorative arts. Since Mr. Downs pioneered in the use*

---

[10] Winterthur Corporation, from the "Minutes" on file in the office of the Director (September, 1954).

[11] From a multilith copy in the files of the Joseph Downs Manuscript and Microfilm Collection (hereafter DMMC).

of this kind of source material—his own book being a brilliant example—I feel that there could be no finer tribute to his memory than to begin a collection of manuscripts in his name.

Such a collection would be a stimulating memorial which would keep alive not only the name of Joseph Downs, but also the exacting standards of scholarship on which he built his reputation and for which he was famous.

                                        Sincerely,
                                        John Sweeney

Touched and pleased that the suggestion had come from such a recently appointed staff member, Mr. Montgomery dispatched a letter to the scholar's sister, Elizabeth Downs, to ask the family's reaction to such a memorial. Soon after, Miss Downs responded that the family was pleased with the idea and that she would like to make a contribution if the collection came into being. Mr. Montgomery then wrote to Henry Francis du Pont, who pronounced the idea excellent. After making some perceptive suggestions, Mr. du Pont volunteered to donate a considerable number of manuscripts from his own collection and also to contribute to a purchase fund.

In January, 1955, the Board of Directors passed a resolution which states in part:

It is the pleasure and intention of this Board to establish the Joseph Downs Manuscript Collection of documentary material, both in manuscript and on microfilm, that scholar and student alike may be inspired by Joseph Downs' example to continue his sound and basic approach to the study of American arts and history . . .[12]

When an announcement was made of the new collection, Mr. William W. Heer, a friend of Joseph Downs and executor of the estate, gave books and papers which had been left to him; the Misses Elizabeth and Agnes Downs gave other reference books that had belonged to their brother, and also contributed to the purchase fund; many others who had known Joseph Downs responded through contributions of documents or gifts of money.

To make a collection that will not only perpetuate the name but also exemplify the scholarly standards of an individual is a difficult task. Yet, when Miss M. Elinor Betts was made part-time librarian in charge of the collection, she took up the new duties with the enthusiasm that characterized all her activities while at Winterthur. Having served devotedly as secretary and editorial assistant to Joseph Downs, she was well acquainted with his methods. She knew the kinds of material he had used, his methods of acquiring these materials and of weaving them into a meaningful text. Miss Betts did all that is demanded of a librarian—purchasing, cataloguing, helping readers. Further, she went beyond the necessities by studying and keeping up with new developments in library and archival methods, investigating the latest equipment and approved storage practices, setting up case history files on documents in the collection and accumulating a list of subjects under investigation by Winterthur students and staff members. But of first importance to Miss Betts was a rigorous interpretation of the purpose of the Downs Collection. In both her capacities as editor and as manuscript librarian, she worked closely with the graduate students of the

---

[12] From a multilith copy in the files of DMMC.

Winterthur Program, helping them to locate and interpret original material, teaching them to cite it correctly and to use it effectively. To encourage use of the Downs Collection she wrote short articles for the Winterthur *Newsletter*. By quoting liberally from early documents which might throw new light upon Museum objects or upon early American customs, she subtly demonstrated the growing usefulness of the collection. Though she never taught a course in the Winterthur Program, Miss Betts was a most effective teacher to the students and Winterthur staff members who sought her help.

As the manuscript collection grew, and as Winterthur expanded and began a more energetic publishing program, Miss Betts found that she could not continue to fulfill her dual responsibilities as editor and as Librarian of the Downs Collection. Late in 1960 a full-time librarian came to take charge of the Downs Collection and Miss Betts returned to her editorial duties. Subsequently she left Winterthur to return to teaching, but not without having left an indelible impression upon the Joseph Downs Manuscript Collection. Following the pattern set by her, the present librarian continues to work closely with Winterthur researchers, especially with the graduate students, instructing them in the use of documentary material in the course of research rather than in the classroom.

When the writer, a person who had not known Joseph Downs, assumed responsibility for the collection, it was necessary to turn to Downs's writings, to his notes and to people who had known him to gain the information necessary in order to fulfill the established purpose of the Downs Collection. In the course of conversational inquiry about Mr. Downs, two comments came forth which seem to be consistent with everything else learned about him. A man who had known and worked with Downs said: "I know it sounds trite, but the only way to describe him is to say that he was a gentleman and a scholar." A former student remembered this piece of advice from Mr. Downs: "The only way I know to learn anything is to go and look at a lot of things." Joseph Downs's gentlemanly way and his scholarship gained for him the respect of other students and scholars and gave him access to fine American antiques and to documents in the hands of private collectors. If he knew more than most students of American antiquities, it was because he strove to see more; because he was allowed to see more; and because he could see more in what he looked at.

The memory of Joseph Downs is still very real to many students and collectors of American antiques. The manuscript collection named in his honor has benefited in many ways from this memory. Many of his friends have become friends of the Downs Collection, giving it valuable gifts and invaluable help. But perhaps more important than the gifts or the assistance is the image the Collection has taken on. In exemplifying Downs as the type of scholar it wishes to serve and wishes to be able to serve, the Collection has achieved a certain personification. It is not just another collection; it is the Downs Collection. Having been insured against the stagnation which might have resulted had it been limited to the *specific* materials Downs was interested in rather than the kinds of information he utilized, the Collection is free to develop as the mind of a scholar would develop. Designed in terms of the scholar, it looks for better ways to serve scholars.

The particular value of the Joseph Downs Manuscript and Microfilm Collection is that it attempts to bring together into one place and to arrange in an orderly fashion all attainable manuscript material that is in any way relevant to the early American arts. In general, the collecting interests have been defined as broadly as practicable. Any type of manuscript or ephemeral material which in any way adds to or documents our knowledge of American craftsmen and artists has been considered desirable. The manuscripts take many forms—account books, bills, letters, shipping invoices, household inventories, trade cards, printed billheads, and the like. In addition to American materials, some English and European sources have been found useful. Much desirable material is already in permanent collections elsewhere, and therefore must be obtained on microfilm.

Only rarely do large bodies of related material come into the Collection. The bits and pieces of the histories of America's early artists and artisans must be patiently accumulated. Eventually, as the Collection grows, the pieces begin to fit together into meaningful patterns. It is not possible, in one brief article, to give any accurate idea of the scope of the Downs Collection, nor is a catalogue of the holdings appropriate here; but perhaps a short account of a number of items that have begun to exhibit some interesting relationships may serve to give an impression of the content of the Collection.

One of the more remarkable coincidences that has come to light in the Downs Collection links Downs, R. T. Haines Halsey, and at least three other students of American furniture—Charles O. Cornelius, Walter A. Dyer and Nancy McClelland—to a nineteenth-century cabinetmaker named Ernest Hagen, who was also the first person known to have taken an historical interest in the work of Duncan Phyfe. Tracing more closely the interrelationships between these individuals could well lead to a fuller understanding than we now have of the development of the study of American craftsmanship as it began late in the nineteenth century. The coincidence came to notice when Winterthur received from Mrs. Halsey a portion of the research notes of R. T. Haines Halsey. Found in these papers was a little notebook, subsequently revealed to be the original manuscript of "Personal Experiences of an Old New York Cabinetmaker" by Ernest Hagen. Only after the manuscript became the subject of an inquiry was it discovered that another, less extensive version of it is among the papers of Joseph Downs, who had evidently obtained it through Walter A. Dyer, author of *Early American Craftsmen* (1915).[13] The story of the untangling of the confusion existing between these two manuscripts has already been told,[14] but while working on the problem, the author noticed that the role played by Hagen in the study of Phyfe has never been fully explored. This topic in turn led to some consideration of Phyfe documentation.

The only original sources for information on Phyfe aside from Directory listings and labeled pieces that were quoted by early writers prior to 1930 included a watercolor-drawing of Phyfe's workshop, a bill from Phyfe to Charles N. Bancker of Philadelphia, dated 1816, and a drawing of two chairs which has always been associated with the bill to Bancker. The watercolor of Phyfe's shop is now at the Metropolitan Museum of New York. The Bancker bill and the drawing of the two chairs were purchased for the Downs Collection in 1956.[15]

---

[13] WALTER A. DYER, *Early American Craftsmen* (New York: The Century Company, 1915).
[14] ELIZABETH A. INGERMAN, "Personal Experiences of an Old New York Cabinetmaker," *Antiques,* LXXXIV (November, 1963), 576-580.
[15] DMMC, No. 56 x 6.3-4.

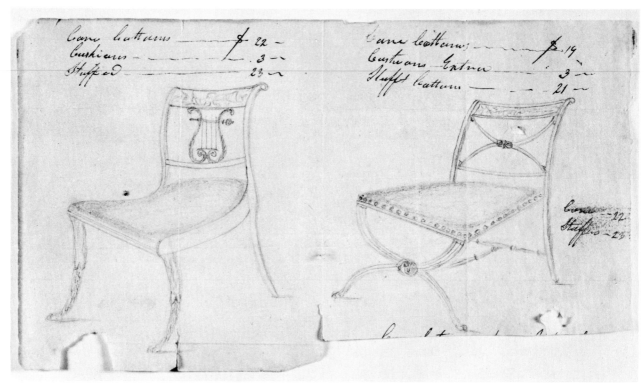

Drawing of Two Phyfe-type Chairs *associated with a bill from Duncan Phyfe to Charles N. Bancker dated August 21, 1816. Pencil sketch, 4 3/8 x 7 15/16. (DMMC 56 x 6.4)*

The often published Bancker bill with its companion drawing is in good company at Winterthur, where are also to be found the inventory of Phyfe's estate,[16] a copy of the auction catalogue of his shop (1847),[17] and several other Phyfe bills. In 1930 an author more commonly concerned with Philadelphia, William M. Hornor, Jr., published an article on Phyfe in which he reproduced a bill from Phyfe to William Bayard.[18] This bill, along with the Charles N. Bancker bill, and another bill issued to George P. MacCulloch were published by Nancy McClelland in *Duncan Phyfe and the English Regency* (1939).[19] The Bayard and MacCulloch documents are now at Winterthur,[20] as is some of the furniture sold to Bayard.[21] In addition, two more bills for furniture made by Phyfe for Thomas Masters are in the Downs Collection along with originals or photocopies of four other documents which mention furniture or coffins made by Phyfe.[22] The

[16] Inventory, estate of Duncan Phyfe, New York, 1854, DMMC, No. 54.37.34.

[17] HALLIDAY AND JENKINS, *Peremptory and Extensive Auction Sale of Splendid and Valuable Furniture, on Tuesday and Wednesday, April 16, and 17, . . . at the Furniture Ware Rooms of Messrs. Duncan Phyfe and Son . . .* (New York, [1847]), DMMC, No. 55.510.

[18] WILLIAM M. HORNOR, JR., "A New Estimation of Duncan Phyfe," *Antiquarian*, XIV (March, 1930), 37-40.

[19] NANCY McCLELLAND, *Duncan Phyfe and the English Regency 1795-1830* (New York: Walter R. Scott, Inc., 1939) pp. 257, 281.

[20] Manuscript bill of Duncan Phyfe, Winterthur Museum, No. 61.1436; DMMC, No. 54.37.33.

[21] Chairs believed to be those described on the Duncan Phyfe bill, note 20 above, Winterthur Museum, 57.720.1, 2; 57.719.1-10.

[22] DMMC, Nos. 61 x 52.1-2, 54.37.40, 54.83.47, 63 x 61, Ph-413.

Downs Collection also has on microfilm a group of privately owned Bancker papers and a small group of bills and letters pertaining to Thomas Masters, a New York Merchant.[23] From the Bancker papers we learn that although the prominent Philadelphian purchased furniture from New York, he patronized at least one Philadelphia cabinetmaker, Michel Bouvier.

Perhaps as a result of his interest in Phyfe, Ernest Hagen seemed to realize that furniture historians would some day be concerned with other nineteenth-century New York cabinetmakers. In his "Personal Experiences" he described a number of cabinetmakers whom he had known or had worked for. Among those mentioned is John Henry Belter, the subject of an article by Joseph Downs in 1948.[24] Ironically, Downs had in his possession only the briefer form of Hagen's manuscript, and thus apparently did not know of Hagen's discussion of Belter and of Charles A. Baudoine, who popularized the Belter style. Downs did have access to the inventory of Belter's shop, which is now in the Downs Collection, as are a number of other inventories of nineteenth-century New York and New Jersey cabinet-makers.[25]

Although Hagen set out to tell the history of his own life, his "Personal Experiences" deal almost as much with the work of other craftsmen as with his own. In his little notebook he mentions many of the early customers of the partnership of Meier and Hagen, but neglects to include an illustrious customer of a later date—Louis C. Tiffany. The records of purchases by Tiffany and by other New Yorkers are to be found in two account books now the property of the New-York Historical Society. These volumes have been microfilmed for the Downs Collection.[26] A printed bill-head of the Tiffany Company showing the storefront about 1862 was given to the Collection recently. Also at Winterthur, though not actually a part of the Downs Collection, is a microfilm of an auction catalogue of the sale of part of Louis C. Tiffany's estate.[27] Undoubtedly, others among Hagen's customers are also represented in the art auction catalogues which have been filmed by the Archives of American Art in cooperation with Winterthur from collections at the New York Public Library and elsewhere.

In the years since 1954, the Joseph Downs Manuscript and Microfilm Collection has grown from an idea to an active part of Winterthur's research and teaching program. The Collection is growing steadily and is being used with increasing frequency. It is hoped that this trend will continue and that future students of the American decorative arts will continue to turn for help to the manuscript library which was established to perpetuate the scholarly ideals of Winterthur's first curator.

[23] DMMC, Nos. M-101, 60 x 24.1-6, 61 x 52-62.

[24] JOSEPH DOWNS, "John Henry Belter and Company," *Antiques*, LIV (September, 1948), 166-168.

[25] DMMC, No. 54.37.34.

[26] DMMC, No. M-465.

[27] THOMAS BENEDICT CLARK AND TIFFANY STUDIOS, *Illustrated Catalogue of a Notable Collection of English Furniture of the XVII and XVIII Centuries. The Collection Formed by Mr. Thomas B. Clark and Acquired by Tiffany Studios . . . Catalogued by Luke Vincent Lockwood.* (New York: American Art Association, 1910). Microfilmed by the Archives of American Art from the original in the Collection of the New York Public Library. DMMC, No. N155.

Fig. 1 Corbit-Sharp House, Odessa, Delaware, built 1772-1774. Restored by Mr. H. Rodney Sharp, 1940, and presented by him in 1958 to the Winterthur Museum.

The Corbit-Sharp House
Family Circle: 1818-1845

By HORACE L. HOTCHKISS, JR.

In 1958 the Winterthur Museum received a sumptuous architectural adjunct in the Corbit-Sharp House in Odessa, Delaware, 25 miles south of Wilmington (Fig. 1). It is a pre-Revolutionary house, skillfully restored and furnished with distinguished Delaware Valley antiques. Its donor, H. Rodney Sharp of Wilmington, had spent many years on this project, starting in 1938, when he acquired the house from the descendants of the builder.

Located on Main Street in the little town of Odessa (formerly Cantwell's Bridge), The Corbit-Sharp House has been endowed by Mr. Sharp and is open to the public under Winterthur supervision. A remarkably handsome example of a Philadelphia-influenced village residence of the 1770's, it has been comprehensively described and its history documented in *Grandeur on the Appoquinimink: The House of William Corbit at Odessa, Delaware* by John A. H. Sweeney.[1]

[1] University of Delaware Press, Winterthur Series book, 1959. References in this article to the lands, houses, and furniture of the Corbits are based on the *Inventory*, the *Wills* of William and Mary Corbit, and other family documents published in this book. Genealogical references are based on the chart compiled therein by Mr. Sweeney and on WILLIAM C. SPRUANCE'S, *The Spruance Family in Delaware, 1733-1933* (Wilmington, 1933).

In his book Mr. Sweeney records the life of the first owner, a Quaker tanner and landowner, notable, it would appear, for his good taste in architecture and furniture as well as for his business ability. In addition, Mr. Sweeney briefly sketches the lives of Corbit descendants through the nineteenth century and into the twentieth.

A house lived in by the members of one family for a hundred and fifty years provides a fascinating scene for a study of American domestic life. Pictures and documents still owned by members of the Corbit family, the publication of which did not fall within the scope of *Grandeur on the Appoquinimink,* allow us to carry forward in detail a phase of the family history: the long widowhood of Mrs. William Corbit.

When William Corbit died in 1818, aged seventy-two, he willed his house to his eldest son Pennell with the proviso that his widow should have life ownership. Mrs. Corbit, who was fifteen years younger than her husband, lived on until 1845. By this time her stepson Pennell had been long dead and her own son, Daniel, had bought the inheritance rights to the house from one of Pennell's daughters. Since the death of his father, Daniel had always been the "man of the house," but waited twenty-seven years to become its possessor.

In August, 1818, when the *Inventory* of William Corbit's furnishings was made, Mrs. Corbit, in addition to Daniel (b. 1796), probably had living at home her two daughters, Sarah (b. 1795) and Mary (b. 1798). The house seems to have been comfortably but not elaborately furnished. Mrs. Corbit probably occupied the crowded bedroom on the first floor behind the parlor. Perhaps the two daughters shared the long drawing room on the second floor which had been converted into a bedroom. Daniel very probably had a "Back Chamber." (A windowless side wall of the Corbit House faced Main Street; back bedrooms overlooked the side of the adjoining property owned by David Wilson, now The David Wilson Mansion, Inc.). Thomas, fifteen, was serving an arduous apprenticeship in Philadelphia, and was probably seldom in Cantwell's Bridge. The Negro servants doubtless included a cook and housemaid and the indentured "Abraham Dorsey" who worked around the place and took care of the horse and two cows.

Mrs. Corbit's eldest son, John C. Corbit, had his own house and farm across the Appoquinimink Creek toward the Delaware Bay. This "Plantation" provided Mrs. Corbit with her firewood. Pennell Corbit and William Fisher Corbit, William's older sons, by previous marriages, also had residences nearby.

In the 1820's Mrs. Corbit lost two of her children, Thomas and Mary. In the meantime, Pennell Corbit had died, and in 1821 his two orphaned daughters came to live with their step-grandmother. Sarah Clark Corbit and Mary Pennell Corbit were a half generation younger than their Aunt Sarah and Uncle Daniel. Daniel had been appointed their guardian, and he also took over the family tannery which their father had operated for years.

Mrs. Corbit's maiden name had been Mary Cowgill. For almost a decade there were two Marys and two Sarahs in the house; the third Mary, Daniel's sister, died in 1826. John C. Higgins, young Sarah's son, of St. George's, Delaware, later wrote: "Those who have been privileged to visit in the homes of the people of the religious sect of *"Friends"* need not be told how blessed these children were in their rearing. The five inmates of the home loved each other with a devotedness that I have rarely seen equalled. While they lived, after being long settled in life, and with children of their own, it was truly a sight worth seeing when they met; they literally fell upon each others' necks in transport of joy and affection." [2]

The household of Mrs. William Corbit was fortunate in having Daniel as "man of the house." Daniel paid all the family bills, arranged for his nieces' schooling, ran the tannery, and supervised the family tenant farms. A miniature of him (Fig. 2), painted probably about 1820, shows a handsome man of firm character. Though he attended Friends' Meeting, he is not depicted in Quaker dress, but wears a smartly cut dark blue coat with brass buttons. As John A. H. Sweeney has told, in *Grandeur on the Appoquinimink*, Daniel was imbued with a feeling for family tradition unusual in a 19th-century business man. Mrs. Corbit had a son who would cherish his father's house and even go so far as to keep its original furnishings together.

Aside from the absences of the girls at boarding school, the family group remained intact until 1830 when the aunt and nieces married within a few years of each other. Sarah Corbit, at the age of thirty-five married Presley Spruance, a future United States Senator, of nearby Smyrna. Young Mary Pennell Corbit married Andrew Snow Naudain and went to live at "Mount Airy" two miles south of Middletown. Young Sarah Clark Corbit married Anthony M. Higgins of St. George's, on the Canal; his family had owned land and farms there for many years. It was the Higginses who jokingly referred to the Corbit house as "Castle William."

In 1833, Daniel, the bachelor uncle of thirty-six, also married.[3] Eliza Naudain, fourteen years his junior, was a "young aunt" of Andrew Naudain. Of Huguenot descent, she was heiress to lands near Cantwell's Bridge. Her portrait (Fig. 3), a small black-and-white drawing now owned by her great-granddaughter, may not do her justice. Her great-nephew remembers her as being "beautiful" in the dark Naudain fashion.[4] The picture, in any event, shows her to have been animated and modishly attired.

The following year, this marriage was blessed with the birth of John Cowgill Corbit, probably named after old Mrs. Corbit's recently deceased eldest son. From a letter written by Daniel to Eliza while she was visiting relatives near Dover, we surmise that he loved his wife devotedly.[5] That he was something of a tease is indicated by the delaying manner in which he reports to her the sex of young Sarah Corbit Higgins' first child—a girl—and by referring to the family as the "O'Higginses."

Daniel, while not inspecting his tannery and farms, was working long hours at his ledgers and business correspondence. In later years his office was a little building located near the kitchen of the house. It may have been there as early as the 1830's. His desk chair by family tradition was a Windsor (Fig. 4).

[2] JOHN C. HIGGINS, *The Higgins Family and its Connections*, MS in the possession of Mrs. Charles Lee Reese, (1917), p. 6.
[3] All these marriages were to non-Quakers. In later years Daniel, a "Conservative," attended Monthly Meeting in Wilmington as Appoquinimink Meeting had gone over to the "Hicksites."
[4] HIGGINS, p. 137.
[5] Dated April 28, 1834. In the possession of Mrs. D. Meredith Reese.

Fig. 2   Miniature on ivory of
Daniel Corbit (1796-1877),
2 7/16 x 2 1/8, c. 1820.
Coll. Mrs. Paul J. Nowland.

Fig. 3   Drawing of Eliza Naudain
Corbit (1810-1844), 3½ x 3.
Coll. Mrs. D. Meredith Reese.

Fig. 4   Windsor armchair,
Pennsylvania (1780-1810).
According to family tradition,
used as a desk chair by
Daniel Corbit. Coll.
Mrs. D. Meredith Reese.

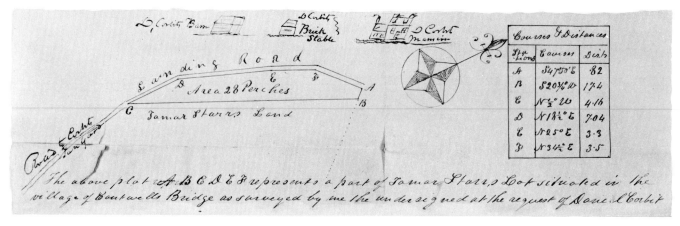

Fig. 5   Detail of survey of "a part of Tamar Starr's Lot," 1839,
showing the tannery road and adjoining Corbit property.
Gift of Mrs. D. Meredith Reese to The Corbit-Sharp House, 1963. (G. CH 63.2)

Fig. 6   View of The Corbit-Sharp House and grounds in 1938,
showing, at left, the old barn before it was torn down.

A surveyor's drawing of 1839 (Fig. 5) contains a marginal sketch of the Corbit buildings, showing the house and, to the left of it, the brick stable and the barn. The barn (Fig. 6) stood until 1938 when, because of its shaky condition, Mr. Sharp felt compelled to tear it down. Running in front of these buildings and finally veering off to the left was the road from Main Street leading to the tannery. The road also existed until 1938, though the tannery had long since disappeared. Daniel had probably enlarged the "Carriage House" mentioned in his father's will to make the barn. He doubtless used it for the cows which grazed on his adjoining properties. The plot on which the Corbit House stood was not large and the place had never been considered a farm.

Inside the house Mrs. Corbit now shared her housekeeping responsibilities with a daughter-in-law; before her death she would see the arrival of four more grandchildren. Mercifully, only one out of the family of four boys and a girl would die in childhood. Mrs. Corbit as a girl in her 'teens had shared the sufferings of the Delaware Quakers during the Revolution. She was surviving into the age of steam-powered transportation, telegraphy, and photography. Her manner of speaking was probably dry and to-the-point, compared to that of her daughter, Sarah Spruance, who was extremely effusive. Mrs. Corbit's step-great-grandson gives us a glimpse of the old lady in the following episode from his earliest childhood:

> *"A cruel mother hen had weaned her chickens and they were huddled in the kitchen shed corner by the smokehouse door. 'Grandmother' Corbit and others were 'in the house' and I was running about the kitchen and shed. Darkness had fallen to some extent and the chickens were hugging each other, when I took a hand. When one of the maids came out most or all of the chickens lay dead. . . .*
>
> *Grandmother was told of it in my hearing. I remember the dreadful sentence — 'Sally that child must be well punished for such cruelty.' "* [6]

Great Aunt Sarah Spruance made quite a different impression:

> *"She admired us for studying our lessons; for reading in the evenings. 'Sally (to my mother) I tell thee thy children are to be intelligent!' "* [7]

Eliza Corbit's death in 1844 at the age of thirty-four must have shaken her mother-in-law. The old lady followed her the next year at eighty-four. Daniel, already middle-aged, bereft of wife and mother, had now to assume a more personal responsibility for his children. He had no way of knowing, of course, that another marriage and years of great business success lay ahead.

In her will, dated December, 1843, Mrs. Corbit had left her daughter-in-law, Eliza, her "New Carpet, & oil Cloth in Back room down Stairs—fringe Notted Counterpane and 'Life of Mary Dudley'—"

Among a variety of other things, including money and her snuff box, she left her daughter, Mrs. Spruance, the "old bed quilt I worked when young."

To the delicate hypochondriac Dr. James Corbit, only child of her stepson William Fisher Corbit, she left twenty dollars in cash. James, like Sarah and Mary Corbit, had been orphaned in the 1820's and must have treasured the time he was allowed to spend with his father's relatives. Quite unconscious, certainly, that Mrs. Corbit dwelt in a monument of Colonial architecture, he looked upon her house as his home when he was not with his maternal grandfather Davis in Smyrna. From a Methodist boarding school in Massachusetts the thirteen-year-old boy had written to his Uncle Daniel in 1827:

> *HUZZA the FRIENDS is the best society there is in my opinion, they can train a child up better, as good anyhow as the methodists. I feel homesick, downcast, melancholy, as if all my spirits is taken away from me. But when I go home I will be joyful and merry as you please. It sometimes seems like as if I was at home setting around your little table. Indeed if I was home I should think it paradise eating Grandmother's bread & butter. O Dear me if I only had the least piece of her nice bread & butter, I would eat it as greedy as a hog. . . .* [8]

---

[6] HIGGINS, p. 22.
[7] HIGGINS, p. 132.
[8] ANTHONY HIGGINS, *The Corbits on Appoquinimink: A Quaker Family of the Border South*, MS in the possession of The Corbit-Sharp House (1941), p. 50.